POSTDATED ROMANCE

POSTDATED ROMANCE

(Until We Meet Again)

Ron Rosewood

Rick and Lisa fell in love. They faced a moral dilemma. Do they act on their feelings immediately and upset their present families, or postpone their romance until they are reincarnated?

CHAPTER 1

FALL 2011

Love is not a straight line from the first meeting to a state of permanent, blissful happiness. Love moves forward, it takes unpredictable turns, it strikes like lightening, or it can gradually evolve over time. Love often retreats as difficulties arise. Occasionally love evaporates like early morning mist. Life without the magic of love would be meaningless.

Was the magic of love in the air the day Rick met Lisa? Was their first meeting a sign of days to come?

Rick, a recently retired office manager, and his wife Meg, had relocated to Duncan, British Columbia. It was the fall of 2011. They had been in town three weeks. One Friday, they decided to have lunch at the Duncan Veteran's Club.

As they entered, the volunteer server smiled "All tables are busy with seats only available on a shared basis. "She nodded her head toward a table for four occupied by two people "Those women are regulars I've seated new diners with them in the past.

Rick buttoned his dark blue sports jacket, squared his shoulders and straightened his six-foot frame as he approached the table. "Good day, ladies, my name is Rick Morrow." He turned sideways. "This is my wife Meg." He paused. "Would you mind if we join you?"

"We don't mind at all, please have a seat. I'm Sheila." She stood to greet them. "I'm in charge of social events." She nodded and turned to her left. "I'd like you to meet my long time friend, Lisa."

Lisa stood to greet the newcomers.

Psychologists maintain that an individual has about one minute to make a favorable first impression when meeting a new person. Rick had kept this thought in the back of his mind.

He was unable to say why that thought surfaced out now, like a flaming arrow, from his subconscious. Standing near the table, he studied Lisa. What attracted him? Was it her shy, whimsical smile that charmed him? On the other hand, was it those round spirited dark eyes?

Eyes shone with enthusiasm as she scrutinized Rick. Lisa stood tall and well proportioned. She gave Rick the impression of someone who had always taken care of her self. Her white blouse highlighted the black pearl-like necklace that graced her long slim neck. The black blazer she wore matched her eyes. Her shoulder length black hair showed just the slightest streaks of silver. Her black skirt hugged her hips in an attractive manner. Her outfit complimented her red pumps and red handbag. She exhibited the picture of a confident woman who took pride in her appearance.

Rick extended his hand, first to Sheila. "It is a pleasure to meet you." He then turned and addressed Lisa with a simple, "Hi Lisa." The fascination between them was instantaneous. Even as he spoke, he sensed that this was a special moment in his life. Holding Lisa's hand, he felt her firm handshake turn soft and yielding. Was she conveying to him a subliminal message of yielding femininity?

With her eyes locked on Rick's face, she gracefully reached out, and stepped forward to greet them. "I'm so pleased to meet you both." Lisa smiled assuredly at both Meg and Rick. Her gaze lingered on Rick as though she also experienced feelings of familiarity.

Rick had the uncanny feeling that they had met each other in the past. His mind restlessly searched for details. Surely, he would remember this striking woman if they had met. He tried shaking off the feeling as being groundless. Yet, he could not dismiss the thought. Had they met before, was it possible? Again, he examined his memory for an answer to explain his feeling.

They had not met in his lifetime, of that he was certain. Perhaps they had met in another dimension. Was this a case of parallel universes or reincarnation? Though intriguing in some aspects, he had always dismissed them so much fantasy, science fiction and mythology. He questioned himself about that now as he gazed intently at Lisa standing there, welcoming him like a long lost friend.

The attraction between Rick and Lisa was apparent to Meg. She motioned Rick to pull back her chair so she could take her seat. Rick obliged, without breaking his gaze with Lisa.

Sheila, noticing the awkwardness of the situation, interrupted the silence. "Please have a seat Rick." She motioned to the empty chair then continued. "Are you two new in town? She turned toward Meg. "I don't believe I've seen you at the club before?"

Meg hung her purse on the chair post. She twisted to face Sheila. "You're correct we haven't been here before.

Three weeks ago, we moved from Brampton, Ontario. We decided to retire to Vancouver Island."

"What prompted you to make a cross country move?" Lisa enquired.

"Rick had a vivid dream about moving here. After some discussions it became clear that it was the right decision at this time in our life." Meg brushed her hair back, "Besides there is less snow here, than in Brampton."

Lisa interjected. "Rick, what did you dream about? Did you dream about finding a gold mine here on the west coast?"

Rick blushed and then regained his composure, glancing at Meg. "I found something better than gold," he joked back, not elaborating any further on his dream.

Lisa leaned back, appearing satisfied with Rick's vague reference, as to what the dream was about that prompted Rick to move out west.

Sheila again tried to redirect the conversation by nodding in agreement with Meg's comment about the weather. "I know what you mean about the snow and cold! I too came out from Ontario ten years ago, from Toronto in fact. Believe me; I don't miss those eastern winters." She pretended to shiver, wrapping her arms around herself to emphasize her statement.

Lisa smiled shyly as she flicked her dark hair back from her face with her right hand. "In my younger days, I spent three years near Churchill. That was enough chilliness to last me a lifetime." She stared at Rick, as though expecting him to respond.

Rick agreed. "I guess being Canadians we're all acquainted with snow and cold. At the time, we accepted it as routine. Now as we get older it is a memory and we want to keep it that way." He laughed, "I still remember the below zero winters in my schoolboy days on the prairies."

Lisa nodded. "I spent a few weeks in Saskatoon on a radar training course one January."

"What year were you there?"

Lisa smiled, "It was in 1971. The year after that I graduated.

"Imagine that, I lived sixty miles east of Saskatoon." Rick was starting to envisage what might have happened had they met at that time.

That is a coincident. "Why didn't you call me?" she said in a teasing manner.

Rick glanced sideways at Meg. "I was preoccupied with Meg at the time." He placed his arm around her shoulder and grinned.

"And with good reason, I might say." Lisa gave Meg a reassuring smile. "From what I can see, you both made the perfect choice."

"We've been married forty years." Meg's face lit up with pride as she finished speaking.

Sheila responded, "You have me beat." She chuckled and then turned and beckoned to the server. "My first marriage lasted all of four years."

They turned their attention to the menu entries. They consisted of a choice between tomato soup with a salmon sandwich or a pasta dish with ham and asparagus. Meg settled for the sandwich combo and Rick ordered the pasta. Rick saw people were having drinks with their meals so he took the initiative raising his arm. The server noticed and came over.

Rick turned to Meg asking, "Would you like a drink, dear?"

"Just a coffee for me please."

The server turned to Shelia and Lisa. Sheila replied with a chuckle. "We'll have our usual three glasses of red wine."

Appearing slightly embarrassed at Shelia's exaggeration, Lisa nodded in agreement and added, "One at a time please." They all laughed.

"Good answer Lisa!" Rick gave her a wink and a smile. "Sure, I'll try a glass of that same red wine." His attention shifted from the server. His eyes locked with Lisa's.

While they ate their meals, Rick and Meg grew more comfortable. Sheila was by far the more talkative. In fact, "a mile a minute" would be an apt description of her speaking manner. Lisa was more reserved. She peeked over her steel-rimmed glasses from time to time, listening intently to all that the others were saying. She had a practiced manner about her. She said she had retired after many years of work as a legal secretary. Absorbing and remembering details were routine to her.

Sheila and Meg provided seventy five percent of the conversation. Rick and Lisa beamed and, bobbed their heads in unison, as Shelia rambled on about the many past and upcoming events around town. Meg described similar events she recalled from the years she and Rick had spent in Ontario.

The topic eventually turned to the next social event. Shelia explained. "I'm promoting a steak night and dance tomorrow evening." She raised her eyebrows. "Why don't you folks join us?" She looked at Rick and Meg expectantly.

Rick glanced at Meg who nodded ever so slightly. He saw Lisa staring at him attentively, waiting his reply. "That sounds like an excellent suggestion Sheila." He looked around the room. "Where do I get the tickets?"

"Over at the bar," Sheila waved to get the bartender's attention. "Brian," she called raising her voice. "We need two more tickets, for steak night." Turning to Rick, she lowered her tone. "Brian will look after you."

Rick took the few steps to the bar and paid for the tickets "Thanks Brian, we'll see you tomorrow night."

Brian smiled as he rang up the payment. "You bet, take care now," he replied with typical bartender feigned sincerity. When Rick returned to the table he handed the tickets to Meg who was standing up, indicating it was time for them to leave.

"Thanks for your company." Meg said.

Rick hesitated as Meg started to leave. An invisible restraint was tugging at his heartstrings wanting him to remain near Lisa, if even for a few more minutes. He turned and smiled gently, focusing entirely on Lisa. "Good afternoon ladies, we'll see you both tomorrow."

"I'm looking forward to it," Lisa countered as she got up and accompanied them for a few steps toward the door. She too appeared to be drawn toward the inexplicable phase where love blossoms.

CHAPTER 2

Throughout the drive home, Meg spoke to Rick and chided him. "You were rather hasty to agree to the dance tomorrow night, weren't you?" She stared straight at him.

Rick had a somewhat guilty look on his face. "I'm sorry honey, but I thought it would be a good way to meet people. We have to start joining in these public events. In a small city like Duncan, only a few things happen each month. Besides you nodded didn't you?" He recalled that he had answered rather quickly when asked about the dance. Was he inwardly anxious to share more time with Lisa? He had to admit the thought appealed to him. He turned quiet waiting for Meg's answer back.

Meg seemed buried in thought for a moment. "If I nodded, it was just a knee jerk reaction, but you're right we do have to get out and meet people. I do not want to appear too eager to join in these events. Let's discuss events between us before we decide." She became quiet and stared out the car window signifying the end of the discussion. She seemed to realize that it was futile to object to Rick's every move. She glanced back at Rick "Let's see how the dance goes on Saturday," she added as an afterthought. Feeling powerless, she again turned and gazed out the window.

"That's the spirit Meg!" Rick replied. He whistled to the radio tune of Johnny Cash's song "Jackson" as they completed the short drive home. It was obviously he was looking forward to the "dance night" event and the opportunity to see Lisa again.

ᖪᖪᖪ

Meg was not amused by the words of the song" Jackson." Were they signifying something ominous in her relationship with Rick? I am just worrying 'about nothing' she assured herself as they arrived home.

Later that afternoon Meg occupied herself with some yard work. As she worked, she continued to be bothered by her recollections of Rick's attentiveness to Lisa. Why should she be worried? Rick had been true to her for more than forty years Was she so insecure that she was envisioning a problem brewing when there was none. She would see how Rick reacted tonight when she turned on her Friday night charm in their bedroom.

ᖪᖪᖪ

Rick spent most of the afternoon on his computer, checking his regular e-mail and the financial markets. He decided to Google 'past lives' to see what he could learn. On one site, he took notice of the wording that in some instances 'past lives are screaming' to be heard. Rick thought of his strong attraction toward Lisa. Was this a past life experience "screaming' to surface? The more he studied the reported true experiences on the site the more convinced he became. Perhaps this was explaining why he had gravitated immediately to Lisa. Could it explain the natural closeness they shared instantaneously? Was this merely wishful thinking on his part?

At age sixty was he slipping into the 'crazy fool' stage that he had observed amongst his fellow male workers and friends in this same age bracket. He thought about it, 'no, he did not feel like a fool. Rather he felt energized by the prospect of developing a new relationship. Was this something that he had to do or was he losing it completely? Had not Meg stood by him all these years. They had a good marriage, and they raised a family together and were now beginning to enjoy the fruits of their hard work. Why even think of anything else but an enjoyable retirement with trips they had talked about and family activities?'

That evening at dinner Rick sensed resentfulness in Meg. She was unusually quiet as she served their evening meal. He had more common sense than to inquire as to what was wrong. That would surely lead to an intense argument. He supposed that the noon luncheon event continued to bother Meg. He promised himself to make it up to her. He decided to break the uncommunicativeness that had developed. "Honey would you like to watch a good movie on TV tonight?" He was hoping Meg would agree to a couple of hours of cuddling on the love seat.

ᖒᖒᖒ

Hesitating momentarily she replied, "Sure, would you check and see what's on, that we haven't seen?" She smiled at the prospect of sharing a couple of hours watching a romantic movie. It would set the mood for the love making plans she envisioned for later that night. She smiled to herself as she stood up and brought dessert over to the table

Rick gathered up the Friday night TV listings and began to scan the offerings. He saw what seemed to be a recent release. "There's a movie called "Date Night" is on at nine," he suggested.

"I've heard of that, it came out last year. It's got Tina Fey in it, hasn't it?" Meg encouraged him to continue.

"And Steve Carell, it says it's about a couple who decide to go on a Romantic getaway to save their relationship." He quoted from the write-up.

"Good, we'll watch how they do that, that from the comfort of our living room." Meg laughed. "The world will look different in the morning." She scowled wondering what impelled her to say that.

Rick was delighted to see her relaxing. "It's decided then. We will watch "Date Night." He got up and cleared the dinner plates off the table, and then started the corn popper.

The evening found Rick and Meg jostling each other on the love seat while balancing a bowl of popcorn on their lap. They had a bottle of red wine and two glasses on the coffee table. The flickering flames of the gas fireplace gave the room an intimate atmosphere.

The movie started out straight forward enough as the movie showed scenes of the couple who seemed to be in a rut struggling with family and work. After they learned of friends that were breaking up due to difficulties, the movie couple went into the city on a special date night to rekindle their relationship. There they were mixed up with strangers who mistook them for someone else. The

situation deteriorated from there but the couple perse-
vered. They rediscovered their love for one another was
still there and stronger than ever.

"That wasn't quite what I expected," chirped Meg as
the credits were scrolling up the screen. She stood up and
turned off the set with the remote. "The ending turned
out well though, everyone was happy."

"They got quite a surprise when those men walked
them out of the restaurant." Rick agreed, referring to
the scene about the mistaken identity. He turned down
the thermostat and switched off the living room lights.
"Don't let it spoil your day," he added as he gathered the
wine bottle and glasses. He took them to the kitchen before returning to the living room.

"Oh it won't do that" she replied as she drew the drapes
"you never know what to expect, do you?" She winked at
Rick as she headed up the stairs to the master bedroom."
Now let's see if we can improve on that ending with one
of our own." She glanced over her shoulder smiling as she
turned at the top of the stairs.

Rick was both surprised and flattered by Meg's direct-
ness. It reminded him of their first few years of marriage.
Those were the happy, carefree days they shared before
the responsibilities of their family and careers began re-
ducing their 'together' time. He attributed the change in
her to the underlying message in the movie they had just
watched.

Without any further thought he joined her upstairs,

carrying with him the morning newspaper that he usually scanned before sleeping. This time he tossed it into the den, deciding financial figures would not be needed that night!

Meg was in the bathroom having a quick shower. After a few minutes she emerged with a bath towel wrapped around her torso." Your turn," she cooed as she reentered the bedroom and walked over to her dresser.

Rick did not hesitate. He was out of the shower in a matter of minutes. As he brushed his teeth he looked at his eyes in the bathroom mirror. 'I've got everything a man could want' he thought, 'why have I got this fascination with Lisa? What could she give me that I do not already have? Where will this end?' The image in the mirror stared back at him looking as confused as he was. 'No help there' he thought. He quickly turned out the bathroom light and joined Meg. Where they going to be experiencing the kind of night orchestrated only in movie scenes?

∽∾∽

Without hesitating Meg encouraged Rick to begin caressing her. They kissed and held each other close. The outside world disappeared. With unfettered enthusiasm they totally lost themselves in each other. Meg masterfully took command, rolled Rick over on his back, and covered his body with hers. She leaned forward and let her breasts meet his reaching hands and his waiting lips. The rhythm of her body sent him deeper and deeper into her and she could feel his every thrust as he responded to her.

The seconds turned into minutes as they reached the place where they both desired to be. They both lay there panting with her still astride him. They relaxed, trying to calm their rapid breathing. They luxuriated together in total bliss. Meg was satisfied that the bond between her and Rick was still strong and steadfast. They kissed several times more as she lifted herself up and over to lie beside him.

᠂᠂᠂

If Rick had tried to envision what Meg had planned for him, he could not have been more mistaken. She came to him with an eagerness that was almost unreal. He realized that this was a new version of his Meg. Gone was the timid, bashful, self-doubting woman that had shared his life for the past forty years. This was a new, passionate Meg and he loved it. He would be a fool not to. What had triggered this change in his wife? As their lovemaking intensified and he was drawn into the common goal of rushing to climax, he thought of Lisa. If this were Lisa, what would lovemaking be like? Would she be this enthusiastic and exciting? Rick felt embarrassed as he forced himself to dismiss thoughts of Lisa. Would there be a time in his life where he could be contented? He put aside all his questioning thoughts. His mind exploded in sheer ecstasy of the moment.

CHAPTER 3

Saturday arrived; the Veteran's Club was a beehive of activity. The dinner was sold out. The Good Times Band was already setting up their equipment. As they entered, Rick glanced around the room while helping Meg out of her jacket. He noticed Lisa's familiar face; she was seated by herself at a table. She smiled and gave them a quick wave motioning them to come over. Rick guided Meg to the table. "Hi there Lisa, how are you this evening?" He smiled broadly as he helped Meg with her chair.

"I'm just fine thanks. You're just in time." Lisa quipped. She ran the fingers of her right hand through her lower locks and turned to face Meg. "How are you today Meg?"

"It's good to see you again Lisa." Meg smiled faintly as she looked around the room.

"I like your outfit." Meg complimented Lisa on her Red Blazer, white blouse and dark slacks. To complete the outfit Lisa again had on her black pearl-like necklace, obviously her favorite article of jewelry.

"Thanks Lisa, is Sheila coming?" Meg inquired as she continued glancing at the crowd.

"She had to drive her husband to Victoria today to a medical appointment." Lisa answered. "I guess the trip wore them out."

Lisa changed the topic and commented, "I've looked forward to this evening. This band is very good."

Meg glanced at Lisa's left hand and saw she wore a wedding band. She had wondered about Lisa's marital status but thought it too brash to quiz Lisa directly. She felt she could find that information out as the evening's conversation and activities progressed.

As they got their drinks, a tall gray haired man approached the table. He was looking directly at Lisa and smiling. "Hi Lisa, may I join you and your guests?" He pulled back a chair without waiting for a reply. It was clear he regularly socialized with Lisa.

Lisa smiled at him "yes Rob I'm sure you can both join us." She gave Rick and Meg a quick glance to gauge their reaction and seeing there was no sign of objections she then continued. "Rob, I'd like you to meet Meg and Rick, they're new in town."

"I'm pleased to meet you both." Rob extended his hand to Meg then to Rick. He took his seat.

"Rob works for the local detachment of the R.C.M.P. here in town." Lisa explained.

"Quick everyone hide your drinks." Rick laughed as he shielded his drink from sight.

Rob smiled accustomed to ribs from the public. "You don't have to worry about me." He laughed as he turned and ordered a light beer for himself.

An hour later with their meal completed and with their drinks renewed they were ready to dance. The band started up. Rick and Meg danced to the country favorite "Rambling Rose."

"You're right about this band Lisa. They sound great," Rick commented as he and Meg rejoined them at the table. The band started their next selection "Amanda." Rick turned to Lisa "Would you care to dance?" He smiled broadly giving away the fact he was expecting an acceptance.

"I'd love to Rick" she replied, without any hesitation. They were on the floor dancing. Lisa was a superb dancer. She prided herself knowing that she could quickly gauge a partner's dance capabilities and then adjust her dancing style to compliment her partner's skill level.

Rick, like most men, had somewhat limited dancing skills, however things went surprisingly well, they danced effortlessly like a well rehearsed couple.

"Lisa you are a terrific dancer" Rick complimented her as they danced smoothly around the room. There was a familiarity developing here that still mystified Rick, he could not explain the closeness he felt towards Lisa.

Lisa replied, "As are you" chuckling as she said it. They both smiled at each other realizing Lisa was well aware of his shortcomings as a dancer.

"That is only because you make it so effortless," He responded.

"Here we are like the Disney chipmunks, giving each other all the credit," she responded they both began laughing.

In what seemed like only a minute, the music was over. They walked back to the table to join Meg and Rob.

"Thank you Lisa. That was lovely." Rick said as he showed her to her seat.

"It was my pleasure Rick." She seated herself as he held her chair in place.

Later in the evening as Meg was dancing with Rob, she discreetly quizzed him about Lisa. "Have you known Lisa long?" she asked.

Rob answered without hesitation, "about five years. She retired here from Victoria."

"Does she have family there? " Meg doggedly pressed for more information.

"I believe she is married. She has a husband. They see each other occasionally. He works as a sea captain and is away from home ten months of the year."

Meg had all the information she needed. She was comforted by the information that Lisa was married, but at the same time concerned that for the most part they were living apart. As she danced with Rob she could see that Rick and Lisa were chatting away with a fair amount of animation. Rick seemed to be making humorous remarks and Lisa responded with smiles and laughter. Meg noted that this was not like Rick. He was usually quiet and reserved in his conversations with women. 'What quality did Lisa have that brought out this exuberance in Rick?' Perhaps she had overestimated her confidence in Rick's loyalty.

As the evening passed, Rick and Lisa had more dances. Everyone seated at the tables near them saw it was clear from their body language that a special bond was forming between them. Meg was not blind to the obvious stares from the other patrons. She promised herself to have a serious talk with Rick.

CHAPTER 4

The next morning as Rick was watching Meg prepare breakfast, his thoughts turned to the forty years they had been together. He had to admit that their marriage was not the perfect marriage. Conversely, neither could he describe their marriage as unpleasant. They had both enjoyed their career opportunities, he as an account manager in an investment firm, and she as an assistant in hospital administration. Meg had taken several years off to bear and raise their two sons. He had to acknowledge that she had done a wonderful job.

Yes, he was indeed fortunate to have had a partner like Meg to share his life. Overall he had to admit he was fortunate for the life he was enjoying and had no regrets.

Meg looked glanced over at him noticing that he was deep in thought. "Honey your eggs are getting cold." Looking at him quizzically, she continued. "Do you have something on your mind Rick?"

"Oh, I was just having a flashback moment, I was thinking about you and the kids over the past years." He took a sip of his coffee and then smiled at her.

"Those kids are now thirty- eight and thirty- six, and have three children between them. You can consider the apron strings as being cut." She warmed up his coffee and sat down opposite him.

"Is Lisa making you feel like a young man again?" I saw

the magic between you last night, as did everyone there." She put a hand on the sleeve of his housecoat

"I'm sorry if it made you feel uncomfortable. Was it that obvious?" He replied with a surprised look on his face. He placed his hand over hers.

"Like a pigeon on a rooftop, but don't worry dear, let's just say you missed your middle age crisis and are having it now, ten years later. In a few weeks we can all laugh at the thought of you and Lisa being anything more than occasional dancing partners."

"I'm sure you are right Meg. I promise you, I will tone things down. After all Duncan is a small town and we needn't add fodder to the rumor mill down at the veteran's club. Thank you for being so patient with me about the whole matter." Rick was hoping he could live up to the promises he had just made.

"We are all human, incidents happen and we have to deal with them as they come up." Meg stood up and gave him a kiss on the cheek as she cleared the plates and cups off the table. She was satisfied that she had registered her feelings about Lisa; Rick seemed to understand her position.

Rick was still thinking about the past twelve hours as he busied himself with washing the two cars. He felt guilty because Meg had to bring to his attention the fact that he had embarrassed her and to a greater extent embarrassed himself at the veteran's club. However he still could not shake the feeling that everything that occurred was unavoidable, almost as if someone had written a script for a scene and he and Lisa were merely performing the scene as scripted. It was as though a director was standing there with them directing every word and each movement as they, the actors, performed their parts.

He continued going over all the traits that he found intriguing about Lisa. Her controlled smile intrigued him. Then her quick outburst to laughter was something he enjoyed. The ever-present sparkle in her eyes was very evident, especially when they discussed activities relating to their youth. They had felt fifty years younger as they danced around the dance floor. Was it so wrong to enjoy each other's company? Should he have danced with other women whom he did not find as alluring? What would be the purpose of that?

His life was advancing into the twilight years. This was the time to enjoy things and relish all that life had to offer. He drove the vehicles back into the garage and put away the hoses. Rick convinced himself that by showing proper respect for his wife's feelings he could still pursue a friendship with Lisa.

Was he merely fooling himself into thinking they could keep from advancing beyond being friends? "Time would tell" was all he could hope for as he continued with his Sunday morning chores.

༒

Lisa was up early in the mid October sunshine as she prepared to clear her back yard of the thick blanket of fallen maple leaves. As she raked the leaves into piles, her dog, a small white bichon female named Puffy, ran in circles and barked at the leaves that flew through the air.

Lisa thought about the previous night she had enjoyed at the club. She realized she had become too familiar with Rick considering they had only been acquainted a short time. She thought back to her husband Eric. She hadn't heard from him for some eight months now. Through the years, the same pattern would play itself out.

Eric would come home after an extended time at sea. They would rekindle the romantic energy between them for a few weeks, and then he would be gone yet again, on another eight or nine month voyage. What worked at first was now becoming an annoyance to Lisa. After so many years spent being mostly apart, she felt disenchanted with the way she had to live her life.

There was no longer any need financially for Eric to keep working. They had discussed that matter many times. However, the sea was in his blood, an addiction you could say. Try as he might he always cut short his leave and went on another sea voyage. Lisa knew it would never stop as long as Eric had his health.

Though they never discussed it, she assumed Eric did have romantic interests abroad. Even if that was the case, she did not want to know about it. He was her husband and he deserved her loyalty. Alternatively, did he? Was it time for her to come to fully realize that fact and perhaps forge a closer relationship with someone who could gave her more than she was receiving

How about Rick, he would be ideal if what she saw and felt so far grew stronger. They seemed to get so much joy from one another when they were close. She looked forward to seeing more of him. Was he the one special man that would put new spark into her life?

What about Meg? Lisa was the type of woman that could not and would not interfere with another couple's marriage. The marriage between Rick and Meg, in all respects, appeared to be a happy one. She swore that she would intrude in such a relationship.

There had to be another solution to her aloneness. What was it? Perhaps time would provide her with an answer to her dilemma.

CHAPTER 5

During the following week a charter bus tour to an Oktoberfest celebration in Port Alberni was advertised in the local Citizen news. It was to be held on the following Saturday night. It was arranged by the local seniors' organization. The tour consisted of a two-hour bus ride to that city. A dinner, dance and other ethnic entertainment related to Oktoberfest would follow, with an overnight stay. A return trip to Duncan on the following morning would complete the event.

By coincidence and unknown to either couple both Meg and Rick booked the trip, as did Sheila and Lisa. As they gathered in the pre boarding area on Saturday morning they greeted each other expressing mild surprise at seeing each other there. Rick teased Sheila and Lisa. "Imagine seeing you here. Are you of German extraction?"

Lisa shot back, "probably more so than you are. Yes, my grandfather was half German." She laughed and continued. "And you?"

"Meg has German roots but never lived there; her grand parents were from Germany." Rick volunteered. "Me, my roots trace back to Hungary."

"I guess we are about even then," responded Lisa. "Sheila, here has English roots, so she rides at the back of the bus with the other non nationals." She turned and smiled at Shelia as she finished talking.

"I dance the polka better than any of you! So there you are." Sheila shot back. She motioned towards the bus as passengers began boarding. They were told the seat numbers assigned to them, as they boarded the bus. Meg and Rick got E 15 and E16. Sheila and Lisa got E 17 and 18 across the aisle from Meg and Rick.

The first part of the two-hour trip was uneventful. Meg sat in the aisle seat, as did Lisa opposite her. They passed the time discussing general things relating to the weather, their grand children, the scenery and the upcoming Oktoberfest. Rick pretended to read the Cowichan Citizen News as he listened to the two women talking. He learned that Lisa and Eric had two daughters who lived in Toronto with their respective husbands. Lisa had a total of five grandchildren, two boys and three girls.

The trip began to get interesting, when at the halfway point there was a thirty-minute rest stop. Coombs was a quaint village with a farmers' market and several other shops. Rick browsed through the bookstore while Meg was in another shop looking at the women's wear. He noticed Lisa scanning the mystery section of the bookstore. "Well look at you scooping up all the Dick Francis novels" He remarked. Lisa turned toward him.

"Francis is the best. Why, is he your favorite too?" She smiled and took a step away from the shelving, turning towards Rick, touching shoulders with him.

Rick smiled "Yes, he is the main author I read." Rick stood his ground enjoying the closeness. Again he was surprised at the similarity of their preferences.

Lisa removed a book from the shelf. "Here is the 'Field of Thirteen,' Francis' collection of short stories. I've read it. It's one on my favorites." She held out the book to him. Their hands touched momentarily, their eyes met briefly. Quickly she looked away, then back again, this time unwavering in her gaze.

Rick smiled "I haven't read that one yet." His eyes dropped. As he opened the book to view the table of contents, he looked back up, "Thanks, I may just take this one," he added.

"You'll like it, I enjoyed it. In fact I still have mine. The story titled 'The Gift' is particularly well written. That is one you will enjoy." They spent the remaining fifteen minutes going through the mystery section and were amazed at the number of common titles they found that they both had read and enjoyed. "It's uncanny." Lisa remarked.

"Great minds think alike" Rick joked. "Why don't you do all the buying of the books from now on? I will get them from you when you are finished. I'll save money," they laughed.

"I have a better idea," replied Lisa. "Let's alternate with each of us choosing a title and then switch upon reading them."

"You're on.'" He replied with a nod, and then continued. "We'd better head back to the bus, or we will spend the evening amongst these books instead of at the dance hall." He chuckled as he stepped aside to allow her to make her way past him toward the exit.

"You and me in here all night "she laughed. "That would make for an interesting evening indeed." She waited by the door while he paid for his book selection.

As they were boarding the bus, the coordinator had an idea. "One person from the set of seats on the left will switch places with the farthest person across the aisle "she announced. "That way we can socialize as we ride along." The plan worked out perfectly for Lisa and Rick. They found themselves seated together for the remainder of the trip.

As the time passed, everything they talked about was magically interesting to the other person. They had the same tastes in music, food, politics, and social justice. They both liked pets. Both had been career office workers. You name it, they could have been twins. They were astounded by how they could almost read each other's thoughts. Neither had experienced such an extraordinary feeling of closeness and kinship.

It was like the culmination of a fifty-year journey searching for contentment and happiness. A close relationship was developing. A relationship was forming that did not revolve solely around sexual attraction, as some relationships do. Rather it was the meeting of two like spirits, coming together, and two floating white clouds connecting in the blue summer sky.

"Rick, we're here!" Meg announced sternly from across the aisle as the bus stopped at the hotel. The passengers began to step down.

Snapping out of his trance like mode, Rick nodded showing that he had heard. He turned to Lisa. "We'll see you over at the hall in about two hours." He smiled fleetingly knowing Meg was monitoring their conversation.

"Save a polka for me." Lisa commented as she stood up and rejoined Shelia.

CHAPTER 6

Meg and Rick took the elevator to the fourth floor; Meg was no longer the self-assured person she had imagined she was. She had seen Rick and Lisa that afternoon warming up to each other. She felt threatened by what she had observed. Was she rushing to judgment thinking that Rick was on path towards a romantic dalliance with Lisa? Was Rick on course for a middle age fling? Was this fantasy of his the beginning of a total mental breakdown? In her forty years of living with him, she had never seen him so preoccupied with someone.

What attributes did Lisa have that she, Meg, could not match or exceed? There were still two more hours until show time. Was it time to remind Rick of a detail or two? If it was female attention he was craving, she would give him all he could handle. She unlocked the hotel room door with the entry card and stepped aside to let Rick go by with the luggage.

～～～

Rick put cases down, then turned to Meg and seeming nervous about Meg's silence, announced, "Here we are, Honey, just you and I."

That was the last straw. Meg snapped back in a demanding voice. "Tell me Rick, just where are we?" She glared at him with flaming eyes. "Where are we and who am I?" She repeated.

Rick hesitated. He knew by her tone that there was a lecture coming. He instantaneously figured out what was bothering Meg." You're my wife." He smiled, and then realizing this was becoming a serious discussion, his face took on a placid look. "I guess you're upset about the time I spent with Lisa on the bus?" He could see by her reaction that he was dead on. 'Perhaps I should not be mentioned the word 'dead' now' he thought.

Meg took a step toward him. He instinctively stepped back and turned sideway to pick up the luggage and lift it into place. "Just stand still for a minute will you?" Meg demanded. He turned to face her. She continued. "Rick, tell me, in the forty years we have been together have we ever let each other down?"

He replied agreeing, "No Meg, I can't say we have."

"How about this afternoon? Don't I deserve some loyalty from you?"

"I'm loyal." He muttered. "What are you so upset about? We were just talking."

Meg continued in a low controlled voice. "I consider your behavior on the bus embarrassing. I can see how you perceive Lisa as an attractive woman. You may have many things in common, or you imagine you do." She stepped back and waved her hand around the room. "This is the real world. Right here in this room is where issues are going to get decided between us. There are no distractions here, unless that seagull on the railing bothers you. In all our time together you have always come to me any time you needed a friendly hug. Why should now be any different? What has changed in the last two weeks that now appears to be pulling apart what we had together all these years?"

She slipped her jacket off and threw it down on the nearby bed emphasizing her frustration. Walking over to the door she rested her hand on the knob. It looked as if she ready to ask him to leave.

Rick stood there dumfounded and speechless. He could offer no defense. Though morally he knew he had not crossed the line, he could not help but agree with every point that Meg had made. He had to atone for the hurt that he saw in Meg's eyes. She stood there with one hand on the motel room door the other on her hip. Was she about to leave?

The seriousness of the situation jolted him into action. He stepped forward and gently put one arm around her and led her slowly over to the love seat in the far corner of the room. Pulling her to him, he hugged her tenderly, feathering kisses on her cheek. "I'm sorry Honey, you're right I acted in an ill-mannered way. Will you forgive me?"

At first she turned her head to one side resisting his overtures. Then she mellowed and cuddled up in his arms and hugged him back. "You're forgiven Rick. Just see that I get the lion's share of your attention this evening." Tears formed in her eyes. Drained of all emotion she sat there motionless eyes closed.

"You've got it." Rick replied, happy to be back in Meg's arms. They shared the next hour cuddling each other.

Rick could still not erase thoughts of Lisa entirely from his mind. If Meg sensed the way he felt, she wasn't revealing it as she drew him ever so close to her.

ᡣᡡᡣ

They arrived as the last shuttle came to take them to the convention hall. By the time they arrived, the hall was filling with revelers. Rick and Meg proceeded to the table that had been reserved for their group and found the last two remaining seats. Meg sighed with relief when she saw they would be sitting several chairs away from Lisa and Sheila.

Rick poured two glasses of wine from the bottle on the table. He sat down and put his arm around Meg's shoulder. They chatted about the decorations and the green white and black Bavarian costumes worn by many of the guests. In short order their meal consisting of roast pork, potato pancakes, red cabbage and cheese noodles, was served to the pleasant sounds of accordion and violin music.

CHAPTER 7

Promptly at seven the Oktoberfest hosts treated the crowd to a display of Bavarian dancers in their traditional costumes. The women wore white frilly blouses with a red and black jumper dress. The men sported white shirts black knee length pants and a black vest. The couples danced a series of numbers not unlike American square dancing. They finished the show with a series of comical skits, the theme of which was two men each vying for the affection of one particular damsel. She in turn pretended disinterested in either of them. In fact, she chose a third man, once the first two suitors made complete fools of themselves.

The festivities then turned to dancing and drinking, with beer being the most fitting and preferred beverage. The dances consisted mostly of polkas, with a sprinkling of waltzes and a few modern tunes for the younger folk. Meg was an accomplished polka and waltz dancer. Rick managed to stay in beat and improvise a step here and there to keep in rhythm with her. Rick stole an occasional glance toward the seats occupied by Lisa and Sheila. He noted that they were not being invited for dances.

Most of the people present were either couples or unattached women, which was usual for an event like this. These function appealed to the 'over sixty' crowd.

Rick was reluctant to approach Lisa for a dance due to Meg's expectations of him for the evening. He knew that

Lisa, of course, did not know about the harsh lecture that Meg had unleashed in room 403 earlier that afternoon. He wondered just what was going through Lisa's mind as she sat there a scant six seats away.

Lisa and Sheila were enjoying the continental atmosphere. They had not attended an authentic Oktoberfest previously, and were taking snapshots of the dancers in their colorful costumes. Lisa, though new to the festival part had always enjoyed the fast pace of polka dancing. She was hoping that she would have a chance to enjoy a few dances. She had noticed the attention Rick was showering on Meg soon after they arrived. She saw them dancing on the floor engaged in the spirit of the evening. That made her feel rather embarrassed as she thought back to the afternoon chatter Rick and she held.

Lisa saw now that perhaps she was being caught up in her own hopes. Was she misreading Rick's apparent interest in her? What she thought were telling signs may be for the reason that he was merely humoring her.

Sheila noticed her deep in thought and made a suggestion. "Why don't we go powder our noses?" she suggested. "Perhaps some of the unattached men in here will see us and approach us."

Lisa agreed. "I'm with you, sitting here is not my idea of a good time." She got up as a short break in the music cleared the dance floor. As they walked down one side of the room they garnered some stares from a number of men. A few minutes later they were back at their places. Music again filled the room.

Their plan had worked, a pair of Bavarian costumed clad gents strolled across the floor. They each held two huge mugs of beer in their hands. The older of the two ventured a comment. "We saw you were out of beer. Can we offer you ladies a share of ours?" He continued. "I'm Fritz and this nobody here is Heinrich," he smiled and broke into a jovial laugh. He placed the mugs on the table in front of the women."

"That is very neighborly of you Heinrich" Sheila replied, as she took a mug of beer and raised it "Skol" she announced as she clicked glasses with the men. Lisa followed suit. Sheila motioned to the men to join them. The music began and Heinrich politely asked Sheila to dance.

Fritz nodded at Lisa and stood up with outstretched arms. "Let's make it a unanimous." He offered his hand to Lisa. She smiled and joined him. As they twirled around the floor, Fritz realized that his partner was an accomplished dancer. He out did himself in trying to match her steps. "Are you from Alberni?" he asked, as they danced.

"I'm from Duncan," she replied. "We came up on a special bus charter just for this event. We will be heading back tomorrow."

"I like Duncan." Fritz added. "Not as isolated as this city. However, I like the inlet and the sea here."

"So does my husband, he's a sea captain. In fact he is out on a trip to Australia right now."

Fritz looked a bit deflated. "I have not travelled that much. In fact I think I've never been more than forty miles away from land."

"We can't all be seamen and navy men" she replied as they finished the dance. "Besides, if it wasn't for you, I would be still sitting at the table over there hoping to get a dance. Thank you very much for joining us."

"The pleasure is mine." Fritz held her chair as she got seated." I see Sheila and Heinrich are staying on for another dance. Tell me, what do you do while your husband is away on his ship?"

"Oh, I like to garden, I read a lot. We have weekly dances in town and I socialize at the Veteran's Club." She glanced again and saw Rick and Meg out on the dance floor. A thought came to her. She turned to Fritz. "Fritz would you do me a small favor? Would you ask the lady in the red dress to dance? I understand she is an excellent polka dancer. I 'm sure you will enjoy dancing with her."

Fritz looked confused for a moment. Then his face lit up as he guessed her motive. "For you, I will do it. After all, this is Oktoberfest, anything goes, right?" He looked at her and grinned. He stood up and taking an indirect path he approached Meg from another side and asked her to dance. Meg appeared impressed with his Bavarian get-up and agreed with a smile.

Lisa glanced up the table and saw Rick looking her way. She nodded towards the dance floor; they both stood up and came together on the dance floor."

Where have you been?" she teased as they began the dance.

"I was waiting for this moment." He replied as he held her close and they began dancing. He felt he owed her an explanation. "Meg was a bit embarrassed about the way I ignored her on the trip up."

"I can appreciate that," Lisa nodded and replied, "I

suppose. I would be annoyed too, if I was in her place. Do you suppose I should apologize to Meg?"

"I'm glad you understand Liza. No, you need not apologize. Let us leave matters as they are. I don't want to bring that all up. I'm sure you agree?"

"Yes of course, we can be friends without disrupting our present relationships can't we?" She looked squarely at Rick prompting him for an answer.

"Why not, we just have to be a little more discreet" He saw her nodding slightly. He made a further suggestion, "do you have an e-mail address, Lisa?"

She raised one eyebrow, then gave him an uncertain, half smile. "It's Lisagirl@Shaw.ca, very easy to remember." She blushed slightly then smiled and added. "When will I hear from you?"

"I'll write every day maybe twice a day," he chuckled as she momentarily believed him. Then she realized that he was teasing her.

The music ended and he walked her back to her seat. "Thank you for the dance, Lisa." She nodded and smiled as he turned and rejoined Meg.

"And how is Lisa this evening?" she inquired as Rick sat down.

"I gather she felt somewhat sheepish about our ignoring you this afternoon." Rick spoke in a half-truth hoping Meg would not get upset.

"Then we all understand each other, don't we?" She gave Rick a stern look. She noticed Rick broke eye contact with her rather quickly. Meg did not talk about it further, deciding not to spoil the evening by making any more accusations.

CHAPTER 8

Sunday morning dawned clear, clearer than most of the revelers' awareness. They dragged themselves out of bed for the nine thirty a.m. breakfast, before boarding the bus at eleven for the return trip to Duncan.

Meg and Rick were among some of the first ones to arrive at the brunch table to help themselves to coffee while waiting for the hostesses to complete putting out the entrees. Sheila and Lisa arrived thereafter and Sheila steered Lisa over toward the table where Rick and Meg were sitting, "good morning, may we join you?" Sheila requested.

Lisa had not divulged, to Shelia, any of the previous evening's conversations with Rick.

Meg took the lead as she nodded and replied, "good morning, yes please join us." Her sincerity was passable. She continued, "How did you ladies enjoy the evening?"

"Very much" Lisa replied, as they took their places. "Those two local men who joined our table made the evening interesting. The music was terrific with the three alternating bands. There was music for everyone's taste."

"Rick enjoyed the skit about the rejected suitors," commented Meg as she looked at Lisa and smiled in a provocative way.

Lisa responded, "She certainly made them look silly. They were, bickering over her as if she were an item at an auction house. I'm glad she settled on the third guy. It gave the other two something to think about." She turned to gaze at Rick. "Don't you think so, Rick?"

Rick was careful in his choice of words. "There was a lesson to learn from that skit. You can't ignore the modern woman." He put an arm around Meg, squeezed her shoulder, and pulled her towards him. Meg obliged by snuggling closer.

The brunch buffet lineup began forming so they all hurried to get in line. The air was filling with the aroma of bacon, scrambled eggs, waffles and toast. Juice and fresh fruit rounded out the buffet. For the light eaters there was a choice of muffins and other pastry choices with unlimited coffee.

During the meal, the discussions turned to the trip home. They overheard Tom , the driver, at the next table announcing that he routinely stopped at a roadside café along the highway to get homemade ice cream. He suggested a show of hands to determine who was interested. Most of the people at the table thought that was a good idea.

Tom said he would speak to the bus hostess about taking a poll of all the passengers before they started out. The waitress brought out urns of extra coffee and tea and encouraged the patrons to have second helpings at the buffet.

Rick saw that Lisa and Meg were warming up to each other. It seemed as though they both regarded yesterday as old news and that today was a brand new day. Rick promised himself that he would stay in the background and not indulge in animated discussions with Lisa. That might be more acceptable to the other passengers, especially Meg.

The hostess of the bus trip, experienced in dealing with incompatible seating arrangements saw that she now had a situation. With the discreet hint from Meg, about Lisa and Rick getting too chummy, she chuckled as she revised the seating arrangements. Lisa and Shelia were assigned seats about three rows behind Rick and Meg. She made further reassignments of seats to disguise the obvious reason for the changes. The hostess kept explaining to the passengers that it was done to liven up with social interaction between them.

As Rick and Meg took their old seats, they discovered that the people opposite them were two seventy-five year old women. They were busily engaged in knitting teapot warmers for sale at the upcoming hospital ladies' auxiliary sale. Meg looked favorably upon the change and smiled at the hostess who glanced her way. Meg was glad she had tactfully requested the change in seating and was pleased the hostess had no problem with the request.

Tom made a head count; he compared the number with the hostess. Then satisfying himself, that everyone was accounted for; he took his seat and piloted the bus out of the hotel parking lot. The bus turned east on the highway heading back toward Duncan. Rick began completing the Sudoku puzzle in the morning Vancouver Province newspaper and enjoying the warmth of the fall sun streaming through the window.

Meg relaxed and began reading her historical romance novel, Vendetta by Marie Corelli it was a story wherein 'Nina quickly recovers from the loss of her husband,

Count Fabio Romani, to cholera and turns to his friend, Guido Ferrari. The pair wants to celebrate their love. However, they are thwarted by the sudden appearance of an old, family friend. He bears a suspicious resemblance to the husband and friend they had buried not so long ago.'

Rick had read that synopsis on the back cover of the novel and now that he saw Meg reading the book, the idea of reincarnation surfaced again from his subconscious. He did not think that Meg's book actually went there because of the short time lapse. The wording he had read reminded him of the idea of reincarnation.

Rick's mind wandered from the Sudoku puzzle. He began fantasizing about reincarnation, and how he might possibly meet Lisa in his next life. It suddenly came to him, *why not meet Liza herself?* It was the perfect answer to all the obstacles in this life. They would be free spirits, so to speak, and be free to fulfill their dreams of togetherness. That was it! They could start fresh, without any constraints whatsoever. He decided to keep these thoughts to himself and see how more interaction with Lisa developed. If their feeling for one another grew stronger, he would divulge the unconventional plan to her.

Rick was shaken back to reality by the bus stopping. Tom the driver announced. "Folks we are taking a twenty minute ice cream break." Standing up he added. "The washrooms are located at the back of the store." The passengers began filing out, some electing to take his suggestion of ice cream cones. Other passengers visited the bathroom facilities. Others chose to stretch their legs in the clear morning sunshine.

Meg spoke as they exited the bus.' Rick, would you get me a coffee while I visit the washroom?"

"Sure no problem," Rick responded. "I want to get some mints. Those eggs at brunch left a taste in my mouth. I'll meet you right out here by the oak tree." He nodded to the right toward a tree with a dilapidated, leaf covered picnic table under it.

Meg agreed and hurried off to the service building. Rick lined up at the counter until the besieged, lone clerk got to him.

"Good morning Rick" Lisa chimed out from behind him. "Its' a beautiful morning, isn't it?" She brushed her hair out of her face.

Rick turned and smiled as he looked into her bright dark eyes. "This is an ideal day for our return trip back. Did you sleep well, Lisa?"

She blushed slightly. She did not want to say that she had been dreaming about Rick and herself being in bed together. "Shelia is a cover hog," she laughed. "She kept me up half the night. However, I will catch up on my sleep tonight, how about you?"

"I slept my usual four hours, then fitfully." he chuckled. "See what old age does to us!" He too, did not want to reveal that his own thoughts about Lisa had kept him awake half the night.

"We aren't old! I like to think of us as experienced, rather than old," she teased him. The clerk motioned him to step forward. Rick got the coffee and mints and went to the sidebar to add milk. Lisa followed him with her coffee and strolled along with him toward the oak tree. As they neared the tree, she spotted Sheila nearby, window-shopping at the gift shop next door. "Excuse me; I'll go keep tabs on Sheila." She smiled and added, "Since they split us up with the new seating arrangements, I'll see you back in Duncan."

Rick responded with a relieved look on his face. "I'll see you at the Wednesday social at the Veterans,' I presume?" He wanted to let Lisa know that he would have preferred more conversation. He held his breath as he gazed at Lisa's tantalizing figure as she turned to walk towards the dress shop.

"I'm looking forward to it." She smiled and nodded. She walked away with her hips swinging. After watching her for a minute, Rick made his way to the picnic table to wait for Meg. He placed the coffee on the table, spilling a small amount as his nervous hand set it down. He detached a mint from its roll and popped it in his mouth. Thoughts of Lisa filled every brain cell. He could feel his pulse rate increasing as he sat at the picnic table wishing he could read his future. Did Lisa fit into the plan destiny had laid out for him? He could only speculate: however, his subconscious mind screamed, yes, yes, yes!

CHAPTER 9

The charter bus arrived back in Duncan at the Veterans'
parking lot and everyone lined up while

Tom the driver unloaded their luggage. Sheila and Lisa's bags came off first.

They waved to the rest of the passengers as they began
to walk to their car. Lisa give Rick a quick, telling, back-
ward glance and smile as she brushed by him. He locked
eyes with her, sensing their connection. Then, before he
could respond in any other way, she was gone, gone like
a shadow.

Since it was a Sunday afternoon, with no planned activities at the Veterans' club, everyone said their goodbyes
and left. "That Oktoberfest was an enjoyable outing Rick,
don't you think?" Meg commented, as they drove the few
minutes to their home.

"It was our first authentic Oktoberfest," he answered.
"I had a very good time. We'll have to go again next year."
As he said that, he wondered, what the next year would
bring. He would give almost anything to be able to see
ahead a year. "Time will tell" he mumbled, absent-mind-
edly.

"What did you say about the time?" Meg had heard the
first word.

Rick had to respond positively. "I said the time will tell
if we can to go next year."

Meg minimized his reply "Why would you say that, Rick? We will only be a year older; surely sixty-one is not out of our reach. What could happen inside of one year?"

"Your right, Honey I should be more optimistic about our approaching senior years." He agreed, but in his mind, he knew one hell of many events could occur in the space of twelve months. No one was shielded from that risk. He added "Look at those women who were opposite us on the bus. They were knitting away at age seventy-five, without a care in the world."

"I'll get us some wool and needles in the morning in case the knitting urge overcomes you," Meg quipped, as they pulled up in their drive. She stepped out and went ahead to unlock the garage door. Rick waited to park the car and unload the overnight bags. "Why is life so full of uncertainties?" he thought. He turned off the engine and stepped out of the car.

Upon entering the kitchen with the luggage, he saw Meg standing by the blinking light of the answering machine. She pressed the flashing button and listened to the first message. "This is Zippy Cleaners, this message is for Rick. Your dry cleaning is ready for pick up."

"That's a relief" Rick joked as Meg repeated the process." I wouldn't want to miss picking up my cleaning would I?

"Just a minute Rick," she answered as she began listening to the next message. It was from Meg's sister in Penticton. "Meg, this is Eva, I have serious news. Dad had a heart attack. We don't know the seriousness of it yet, but he's been in the hospital since Saturday morning. We will know more on Monday. I'll call you back then."

Meg turned to Rick and reached out. "Talking about bad news!" she exclaimed, "Did you hear that?" It was all she could do to hold back her tears.

"I'm sorry to hear that, Honey," Rick walked over and held her for a moment. "I like your dad. We'll call Eva right now and see if there has been any change since her call." He held for a moment longer. Then he dialed the Penticton number and handed Meg the phone.

Meg got straight to the point "Hi Eva, we just got home from Alberni. How is dad doing today?"

"Hi Meg, I'm glad you called," Eva hesitated. "Actually, we were up at the hospital this afternoon. We just got back in fact, and dad is resting much better." She paused. "The young intern on duty says it may not be as bad as they first thought. They had injected some new drug right away and that minimized the damage. They will be ultra sounding him in the morning."

"I'm glad to hear that. Do you think I should come up to Penticton, Eva? " Meg offered.

"I don't think so, wait a few days, he should be coming home. Come then if you wish. I think he would be more at ease once he's home rather than there at the hospital." Eva was quite convincing.

"Well, I'll consider it tonight and then I'll call again tomorrow say around two," she promised. "Meanwhile, call me if there is any change for the worse" she pleaded.

"I'll do that Meg." They ended the call.

Rick had heard only Meg's side of the conversation." How bad is it?" he enquired, looking concerned.

"He had a heart attack, but he got medication right away so they think he may be O.K. they will run some tests tomorrow morning." She sounded more relaxed as she repeated the information.

Rick could only add. "I'm sure he will be fine. He's always looked after himself."

"Well at age eighty five, we all know what could happen." She shuttered as she realized what she had said.

⌇⌇⌇

Rick retired to the den and sat down in front of his computer. He did not turn it on. He felt sad about his father-in-law's medical problem. In addition to that, he was annoyed with himself for the feelings he felt for Lisa. Looking back on the past two days, he could see that he would never consider disrupting his present family situation, to the point of leaving Meg.

He thought back to when he had first started courting Meg. Her dad Carl had been suspicious of Rick's intentions, like most fathers are. However, within short order he had grown fond of Rick. As they spent time together, fishing, golfing and taking joint vacations, a bond had developed between them. That bond was even stronger than the one between Rick and his own dad. Rick realized that this was his place in life. He would enjoy his family right to the end. Standing up he went back into the kitchen to console Meg. She responded by pouring two cups of freshly made tea.

⌇⌇⌇

Lisa arrived home to an empty house. She had dropped Sheila off at her apartment and had picked up Puffy from the kennel. The dog was overjoyed to see her and kept close to Lisa as she brewed a cup of coffee. She thought about the weekend and the pleasant couple of hours she had spent with Rick. That prompted her to check her answering machine to see if her husband, Eric had possibly called her. There were no messages at all.

She sank wearily into an easy chair with her coffee and looked around at the emptiness of the room. It wasn't empty as far as the furnishings were concerned. Every possible space had a settee, or a coffee table or other finely finished piece of furniture. Expensive paintings and family pictures adorned the walls. The living room was a showcase of opulence.

The feeling of emptiness stemmed from the loneliness she felt. Even though she was surrounded by everything material, she missed her partner. She could hardly call Eric, who was home only about sixty days a year a sharing partner. When he was home, he went golfing four times a week. She thought, what kind of life am I living anyhow? Even a chicken in a farmyard was getting more attention than she. Had her life deteriorated to the point where even a lowly egg laying bird was happier than she was?

She remembered that she had given Rick her email address. She went into Eric's den and cursed him, as she surveyed the desk. It had gathered a layer of dust indicating the several months he had been away. He did not like her to disturb items on his desk when he was away so she kept the dusting to a minimum. She reached over and turned on the computer. Sitting there watching it spring to life, she thought how good life would be if she could switch her life on and off like an electronic gadget.

The screen steadied on the Yahoo home page. Hopefully, she clicked on the mail tab and saw that the only message there was for Eric. It was from his ship's head office. She became curious. "Why would they be emailing Eric, when he's there in their employ? She decided to open the email.

It was from Eric's company's head office. She was shocked at the contents. It read" Captain Eric Johnson, we are confirming that as of October 31, you will be retiring from our service, as you requested. We will be placing you on a full pension. Please accept our congratulations on having served us so well in the past thirty-five years. Yours truly, Robert Browning, Vice President, Personnel."

Lisa found the e-mail to be confusing. Why had Eric not called her and told her that he had requested retirement? It was already November 7. What game was he playing? Was he hiding something from her? Did he have romantic plans with someone else? She deleted the message both from the mail and the trash bin. She would wait and see what he said when he eventually made his appearance. She could not decide whether this was good news or bad. Would she have her husband of thirty years back as a steady and faithful partner? Would he shock her with some other mind-boggling news?

ᘐᘐᘐ

Monday morning dawned grey and showery, as Meg decided to get up. She had not slept well. She had decided that she would travel to Penticton to see her dad. It was a mere one hour flight from Victoria to Kelowna and then a fifteen minute shuttle flight on to Penticton.

Rick awoke to the sputtering sound and smell of brewing coffee. He saw it was only six a.m. After putting on his bathrobe, he hurried out to the kitchen. "Good morning Honey, you're up early" he said, as he pecked Meg on the cheek.

"I couldn't sleep. I couldn't stop worrying about dad," she explained. Then she continued "do you mind if I fly up there tomorrow for a few days? You could drive up Friday and stay a couple of nights. We could drive back together on Sunday." She put some bread in the toaster.

"No, I don't mind, in fact that sounds like a good plan. We'll see how Carl is when you call there later today. If he hasn't worsened, then go as you said." He poured himself a cup of coffee and sat down at the table. "I can drive you down to the airport tomorrow morning."

Meg seemed to brighten at the prospect of visiting her Dad. "Let's go to the market and get a few items for your meals while I'm away."

Rick who was quite capable of cooking meals agreed. "I can easily manage from starving for a few days" he joked. "Besides on Wednesday the Veterans 'Club has a good variety of finger food. I can cope very well." His thoughts again turned to Lisa at the mention of the Veterans' club. "Would Lisa be there as she had said?" He hoped so. They could have a couple of hours to talk. He was looking forward to Wednesday. Rick began to daydream about Lisa.

Meg's voice snapped him back to reality, "Don't forget to water the houseplants on Friday morning before you leave here," she suggested. She placed a serving of toast before Rick and then sat down opposite him.

"I'll make a note." He smiled at her. This was an on-going issue between them. He always made notes. She constantly chided him saying it was not good for his memory to have to have reminders to rely on. This time, with more important issues on her mind, she let the matter slide.

Soon they were down at Safeway in the produce section. Rick sorted through the Spartan apples while Meg was selecting bananas across the way. Rick felt a presence near him. Turning slightly to his right, he saw Sheila heading his way. "Well if it isn't the Veterans' nightmare," he joked, as he grinned at her. "And where is your shadow?" He asked referring to Lisa.

"Hi Rick. Yes, it's me the nightmare" she answered." My shadow? "You mean Lisa? I called her earlier. She said she was expecting a call from her husband. She decided to do her shopping this afternoon." She began sorting through the Golden Delicious apples. "I think Eric is on his way home," she added. She bagged and weighed her fruit.

"That's great!" exclaimed Rick, with a less than enthusiastic tone. "I'm sure she will be happy to see him after several months apart."

Shelia expanded on the situation with Lisa. "Lisa sounded apprehensive. She thinks Eric is being forced to retire. She's worried what frame of mind he will be in when he returns home." She began pushing her cart away.

"Tell her we said hi, if you see her, Shelia." Rick said as she carried on.

"Will do, I may see you on Wednesday then, at the social. Are you and Meg coming?"

"Meg will be out of town, visiting her dad; I expect to come down for a short while." Rick assured her. He turned and rejoined Meg.

"I saw you talking to Shelia. What were you chatting about?" Asked Meg, she frowned at Rick.

"Mostly about Lisa, apparently Eric is on his way home." Rick had no reason to hold back that information.

"Well, that is good news. I would like to meet him," exclaimed Meg. She appeared to be comforted by the fact Eric would be back home with Lisa.

"By the time we get back from Penticton he may be home." Rick added. He had mixed feelings about Eric, after the gossip about how Eric never seemed comfortable when at home. They went to the check out counter. Neither of them said anything further. Rick decided he would e-mail Lisa to let her know they were thinking about her.

After two o'clock Meg called her sister Eva. After the preliminary hellos she asked. "How was dad this morning?"

"He's doing just fine. The doctor thinks he can come home on Wednesday if the tests and ultra sound come out as expected." She sounded relieved.

Meg answered, "I'm glad to hear he hasn't worsened. I'm flying up Wednesday and Rick is driving up on Friday. Is that o.k. with you?"

"I don't see why not. If there is any change in dad's condition, I will call you." They continued to agree on details about Meg's visit.

Meg turned to Rick. "Eva said Dad is stable and she thinks a visit will be good for him."

"Well it's all arranged then. I'll go and book your flight for tomorrow morning." He stood up and filled his coffee cup before heading for the den. Once there he quickly booked a flight for Meg with Pacific Western Air leaving Victoria at ten a.m. and after the change of planes in Kelowna, Meg would be arriving in Penticton at noon. He printed out the confirmation sheet, after paying for the flight with his Visa. He emailed Eva the details.

He was about to go offline when his thoughts turned back to Lisa. He e-mailed her, "Hi Lisa. I saw Sheila at the market. She told us about Eric coming home. I just wanted to say we are looking forward to meeting him. I will see you at the social. Meg has to be out of town that day. Cheers, Rick."

Rick felt strange as he glanced toward the den door. He could sense that his feeling for Lisa was growing stronger with each passing day. Where would this all end he wondered? He turned off the computer and left the den "Life is one big jigsaw puzzle he mumbled." He closed the den door with a firm pull.

CHAPTER 10

Lisa couldn't dismiss the e-mail news about her husband's retirement. She decided to remain near the phone on Monday morning. Morning was usually the period during which Eric called, on the rare occasion that he did call. The phone rang at nine thirty. She hurried over and checked the call display. It was Sheila. She answered. "Good morning Shelia, how are you?"

"Just fine thank you." She answered. "I'm just wondering if you want to join me on my weekly shopping trip to Safeway." They usually shopped together.

"Not today Shelia," Lisa hesitated and took a deep breath. She had to talk to someone. She decided Sheila was the person. "Listen Sheila that email from Eric's company is still bothering me. I'm staying home this morning to see if he might call." She sounded uncertain and shaken as her voice quivered.

Sheila hearing the concern in Lisa's voice, asked. "What is this all about Lisa?"

Lisa let it all out "As I mentioned, the e-mail informed him of his retirement some days ago. So far, I have not heard from Eric himself. I don't know if he's busy, hurt or just goofing off." She paused.

Sheila reassured her, "I'm sure he'll call in a day or two and explain it all to you." She paused, "let me know if you need anything. I'm here to help."

"Thanks Sheila you're a good friend." As she ended the call, Lisa still felt less than optimistic about Eric's tardiness in calling her. It was not like him to ignore her to this extent; something had to be wrong, terribly wrong!

Lisa decided to check the e-mail again later that day. There was a message from Rick. As she opened the e-mail she thought about the magic they shared a few days earlier. Now she wondered if that feeling would carry over to the Wednesday social. She was looking forward to learning more about Rick. Did he share the same feelings for her? She had a sudden impulse to reply to his e-mail. "Hi Rick, thanks for your message. I have a rather brave suggestion to make. Perhaps request would be a better word to use.

I have received a rather confusing e-mail from my husband's company. I need to talk to someone about it, preferably a man such as you. That way I can get an opinion that is not from a woman's view. I would prefer to do this in a private setting. If you are willing to help me out, I am inviting you to lunch on Wednesday say at noon. That gives us almost two hours before the social." She hesitated for a moment. Was she too brash to make such a request? She decided to do it anyway. She hit the send key.

Tuesday came and Tuesday went. She still had no word from Eric. Wednesday morning's silence produced even more worry. Lisa checked her e-mail and brightened as she opened the reply from Rick.

"Hi Lisa, thanks for your email. Yes, I will be happy to discuss your concerns and offer my opinion on them. Keep in mind that I may come through as sounding biased. I admire your spirit, so you may have to discount some of what I may say. I'm looking forward to having lunch with you and sharing your company. I will see you at noon.

Lisa smiled as she scrolled to the second paragraph. It read, "By the way I have been looking into reincarnation theories. Now, I may sound completely idiotic. However I think that two people who really care for one another, I won't mention any names here, could perhaps meet in the next life and become more than friends. If we have time, we can discuss this in detail on Wednesday. Your friend Rick"

Lisa smiled at the last paragraph of the e-mail. She began daydreaming. What would life be like as Rick's partner in a future life? What if he was a sea captain like Eric was now? Would she be stuck in the same boat? She smiled at her choice of the word 'boat.' What country would they be living in? Would they have children? Would he find her attractive as her new self? Would she find him attractive? Could such a meeting ever happen? Was this postdated romance just so much make-believe? For a few minutes she luxuriated in the dream world of fantasy. Perhaps it was not fantasy.

She took time to read about some reincarnation reports appearing on the internet and became fascinated with the amount of material she found supporting the theory. She read numerous credible accounts about reincarnation. The more she read, the more achievable it all appeared.

This was no longer merely fantasy. There was definitely some foundation to the whole concept. Reincarnation was the basic doctrine of major world religions for thousands of years. She concluded there had to be more science than fiction involved in the reincarnation theory. She went offline and returned to reality. The reality of the emptiness she had to put up with day after day. She shuddered as she looked around her silent lonely living room.

Lisa gave further thought to what she would serve for lunch. She wanted to have minimal work to do while Rick was there. That way they could concentrate on more talk. She settled on salmon sandwiches together with a potato and egg salad. Tea and mincemeat tarts would take care of the dessert.

It was approaching ten o'clock. She showered, dressed, fixed her hair and carefully applied her makeup. She felt exhilarated at the prospect of seeing Rick, as she went about the task of preparing the meal. The radio was playing old favorites from the 1960's and 70's as she went about her work. By eleven thirty she had everything ready. She went into the living/dining room and set two places, including wine glasses. As a final touch, she turned on the gas fireplace and the TV on the music channel.

She smiled as she turned and surveyed the comfortable atmosphere she had created. It had been several months since she had entertained anyone in her home. It felt good to know someone in this busy world had made time for her. Knowing that it was Rick made her feel even better.

The doorbell rang. She hurried to the door. Through the window, she saw Rick's car was parked across the street and two houses up from hers. The doorbell rang again; Puffy started barking up a storm. Lisa instinctively arranged her hair and smiled as she opened the door. "Hi Rick, how are you?" She stepped back to let him by. Puffy grabbed Rick's pant leg and began growling as she tugged and pulled his cuff.

Rick stepped forward dragging Puffy along with him. "What a cute dog you have there Lisa!"

"Well hardly cute, Eric taught him that crazy habit." Lisa said, as she bent over and gently cuffed Puffy. "She's learned to hate ringing doorbells

Rick brought his left arm up and handed Lisa a simple bouquet of yellow daffodils. "Look what I found on your doorstep!" he exclaimed with an impish smile.

Lisa was delighted by the thought. She gave Rick a brief hug, as he stepped forward into the foyer. They held each other momentarily. Puffy started barking again, prompting Lisa to step back. "Thanks for coming Rick. I really appreciate this chance to talk to you." She took his jacket and motioned him to proceed up the stairs. She put Puffy in the garage, much to the disappointment of the whining little terror.

"Like I said, I hope I can help." Rick smiled at her as she neared the top of the stairs. "This is very cheery" he remarked as he surveyed the dining room, fireplace flames and soft music.

"Thanks Rick," She motioned to the table. "Have either seat. I have everything ready. I'll be back in a minute." She turned toward the kitchen, flowers in hand.

Lisa returned a few minutes later. "Rick, would you care for a glass of wine?" she said smiling as she set the flowers, now in a vase, on the table.

"Thanks" he replied "a glass of wine would be great. Can I help you with it?" Rick offered as he stood up.

"I have a bottle of gewürztraminer on the kitchen counter. Please could you open it while I serve the food?" She led the way.

Rick followed her to the kitchen, picked up the bottle and examined it. "I have to admit I am not a wine expert" he commented as he started to open the bottle.

"The name means "spicy" in German. The wine comes from the Alsace Lorraine area." She added. "It is a good wine to have with fish and a good beginner's wine. I'm sure you will enjoy it." She flashed a smile at Rick.

"I'm sure I will," he replied. He carried the bottle into the dining room and poured a full measure in both glasses. Lisa placed the two plates of food on the table.

"I'll be right with you, Rick." She said over her shoulder. She went over to the stereo and put on a Floyd Cramer CD. The first selection "Last Date" started playing as she joined him at the table.

"A toast to the chef," Rick smiled, raising his glass.

Lisa laughed and raised her glass." Sandwiches and potato salad don't qualify me as a chef." She completed the toast and they sipped their drinks.

Rick, set down his glass and nodded his approval. "I can see why you like this wine. It does have a spicy flavor."

Lisa passed the plate of sandwiches to Rick. "Yes, Eric brought that wine home on his last trip." The mention of Eric brought up the reason Rick was invited or presumable the reason.

"Yes Eric, you mentioned you had some concerns about him?" he looked squarely at her. Rick could hear the tune "Sweet Dreams" playing in the background.

She blushed slightly as she described the e-mail that had been received from Eric's company. "I can't understand why he hasn't phoned or arrived home yet?" she said. She took another sip of wine and glance to gauge

Rick's reaction. "It has been ten days since the announcement. It's not at all like Eric to keep me in the dark."

Rick hesitated a moment, while formulating a sensible answer. "Well, here is what I would do. I would suggest you phone or email the company and see if there was any change in their plans for Eric. Perhaps something happened at the last minute, which may have delayed him. By the way where are they headquartered?" he asked.

"London, England" Lisa replied, then continued." "It's nine thirty in the evening over there. I will phone in the morning. It's just so unsettling to sit here having to worry about such matters."

"Lisa, I fully understand." Rick took another sip of his wine. "I too like certainty; we are alike in that respect." He wondered, as he gazed at her. Was this matter with Eric was her sole reason for inviting him over? He waited for her to speak.

"Thanks Rick, now I know what to do in this life." She decided to change the subject of their conversation. "Let's discuss your reincarnation theories. I have thought about what you said and researched it." She hesitated to find the right choice of words. "I really think you and I would have hit it off if we had known each other years ago. Where were you forty years ago when I needed you?" she teasingly asked him. The musical strains of 'It's Only Make Believe" were playing.

"Now, let's see, that would have been 1967." Rick hesitated, "I was twenty-five and single." He smiled thinking of those carefree years of the sixties. The CD was now into Patsy Cline's 'Please Help Me I'm falling.'

She had a quick reply "It would have been perfect. I

was in my last year of university at UBC in Vancouver. It's a shame we didn't meet at that time."

"And me, I was less than an hour away. Isn't life strange? We were so close and yet never met? In fact, I wrote my accounting exams at UBC for six consecutive years. We very well may have passed each other on the campus!" He gave Lisa a pat on the shoulder

"Why didn't you say hi?" She joked as she smiled back at him.

"I expect I was too busy, worrying about the exams, to look at women," Rick teased back.

She admired his easygoing manner. "Seriously now," she stared at Rick with a hopeful look. "What do you suppose are our chances of actually meeting in the next life? The idea intrigues me."

"Statistically speaking, I can't say. I'd like to believe that if we both want the same outcome; our motivation would insure that our chances were excellent. The real key to all success is to have a plan and the motivation to see it through to completion. Everything should start with a plan, wouldn't you agree?" He looked deep into her dark sparkling eyes as he poured more wine.

Her eyes met his straight on signifying agreement. "You can count on me then Rick, I'll be there."

"I'll be waiting for you Lisa. Let us hope it doesn't take too long." They simultaneous raised their glasses and confirmed their pledge. "Always On My Mind' played in the background.

Lisa stood up and began clearing the table

Then Rick could no longer hold back. He stood up and took a few steps toward Lisa. She sensed that Rick was making an advance. Lisa put down the plates and raised her open her arms and moved nearer to meet him. Their bodies joined in the tight embrace. Their lips found each other. There was no question about what was happening to them. They could no longer hide their feelings. For several minutes, they shared kisses and hugs to reinforce their feeling of love.

Lisa found the will to step back. "Rick I think we have to take a time out here." She rearranged her hair as she turned back to the table and again began gathering up the plates.

"You're right, of course." Rick give her an approving pat on her shoulder as Lisa stepped away.

"Are we still going to the club?" she cooed, as she glanced at the wall clock and was about to turn toward the kitchen.

"Why pass up an opportunity to party?" Rick winked, as he replied. "It could be our last chance to socialize." A strange premonition came over him, as he said that. "I'll meet you at the club in half an hour. We can to work out the details of our reincarnation plan."

"I'm not sure I can wait sixty years." She teased as she walked him to the door.

"Let's try" he nudged his shoulder against hers in the narrow stairway. They exchanged a final kiss before he opened the door and stepped outside.

Rick fantasized about their future as he left Lisa's house and drove toward the Veteran's Club. In his heart he knew that Lisa was that special person every man hopes he will find to share his life.

Lisa was buoyed by the affection she had shared with

Rick. She decided she had worried enough about Eric for one week. After all, it had now been eight months since he left. She had received only two calls during the first two months and nothing since then. What kind of a relationship was that?

She put her thoughts to one side as she readied herself and followed Rick a few minutes later.

She arrived and saw him at the bar ordering a drink. As he walked across the dance floor he noticed her signing in and walked over to greet her." Well here we are as planned." He smiled and led her over to a table for two. The Wednesday afternoon socials were poorly attended so there was ample room to secure a table in a quiet part of the lounge. "Would you like a drink from the bar?" He asked in a soft calm soothing manner as they selected a table.

"I see you're having red wine. I'll have the same, a Merlot, if they have it please." She replied. It was her favorite drink. Again, she noticed the similarities, not only in the drinks but in the suitability of table they chose and the way he dressed neat and conservative, not gaudy, the same as her. She glanced around to see if Sheila was present. There was no sign of her. "Good," Lisa thought. By having Rick to herself, they could discuss matters openly and in detail.

Rick returned, "Here you are gal." He placed her drink in front of her and sat down directly across from her. In a low, just barley audible voice he raised his glass "Here is a toast to a long friendship in this life and a perfect life together in the next" He extended his glass just a few inches forward motioning that she do the same.

Lisa picked up her drink and with clicking glasses, replied." That means a lot Rick. It's what I need to hear right now." She took a long sip of her wine, looking up; shed gave Rick an admiring smile, as she set down her glass. Except for a single tear in one eye, she looked at ease. At ease, like a person who knew she was with someone who enjoyed her company. Someone who cared about her. Here was a person who preferred to be with her, not thousands of miles away.

Rick sensed this was the continuation of something special between them. Life was good. Were they casting the die and taking their first step toward their world of tomorrow?

CHAPTER 11

The dance music started. Rick and Lisa danced every number. The magic that had surfaced between them on the weekend bus tour, as well as at their meeting at the bookstore, was resurfacing. Together with the Oktoberfest festivities, their feelings sprung to life at the social. Two magical hours flew by. They were in another land, almost in another dimension. Oblivious to the other people around them, they only had eyes and time for each other. Their bodies moved closer to each other as they swayed to the slower tunes.

Not all this mutual admiration between them went unnoticed by the other patrons, especially those that knew Lisa. Other regulars were raising eyebrows as the afternoon social progressed. As in all budding relationships, there were good-natured comments flying back and forth between the patrons. Rumors were flying like kites in March winds.

Laughing at small hints that he was "sweet on Lisa", Rick ended any speculation by promptly dismissing them with the comment. "Should I dance with someone I don't like? What is the point of that?" That kept the gossipmongers busy, further fueling their imaginations and speculations.

Rick and Lisa were both in committed relationships. Neither of them wanted to or would ever consider ending. They had to defuse the situation. They agreed that they would only see each other at social functions around town. They would be content with just admiring each other, from a distance or across a table. They would have to be at ease to be in the same room together, act nonchalant, and keep at a discreet space between when dancing. Intentions were not actions and they were not certain if they could accept being apart.

This dilemma magnified itself as the afternoon went by. Something had to give. Rick and Lisa concluded that if they were at liberty to proceed based on their feelings, it became obvious to each of them that a serious relationship would most certainly develop. Rick quickly began pursuing the reincarnation theory. Deciding to reopen the subject and get Lisa's opinions, he asked her opinion. "Say, Lisa, I have an ingenious idea. What if, twenty-five years after we die, we reincarnate? Then we can find each other again. That way we can look forward to be together." He raised his eyebrows anticipating a response.

Lisa, after thinking a moment to grasp the concept, she responded with a wink. "What a shameful idea!" She was silent for another moment as Rick's suggestion registered with her. She continued. "Actually, I like it. Tell me who goes first, you or me?" She laughed, as she realized the absurdity of her comment.

"Let's flip a coin." Rick shot back, with a smile." Of course, we'll let nature and fate decide that! We have time on our side. We aren't going to jump off a cliff together now are we?"

"No, the cliff idea is not for me. I prefer the natural way!" she replied, "besides heights scare me." They laughed and had another dance to 'Please Release Me.' the proposed solution began to grow on Lisa as well. It was the only sensible solution to achieving their togetherness. On the dance floor, they quietly explored the chances. For all intents and purposes, someone seeing them chatting on the dance floor would think they were merely chatting. Like two people talking about the quality and price of produce down at the farmers' market.

"There is much to consider, many details have to be worked out. Where will we meet?" Rick said then answered his own question. "Of course we have to pick a site that will be in existence in the future. I believe Niagara Falls would be ideal. What do you think Lisa?"

Lisa responded. "That sounds like the ideal place! Not only is it a permanent landmark, it also has the perfect romantic setting for such a happy reunion." She finished with, "besides I've never been there." They both laughed at the inference of her having to wait until the next life to see the Falls.

Rick had further thoughts. "Let's make it between July 1st and July 4th. That would be the most likely time people would be visiting Niagara Falls. We'll try to meet there in 2075 and every year thereafter until we find each other."

Lisa asked "How will we remember the chosen site?" She answered her self. "This question poses a little more of a problem. I think that if we remind ourselves of the location daily while we are still alive, then we can recall the information into the next life."

"That is a brilliant idea," see how ideas are forming in such an easy, manner." In his mind, their plan appeared more and more possible, believable and exciting. Rick continued. "How will we know each other?"

That is a no brainer" Lisa quipped "I am sure we will instinctively know each other the moment we are within fifty feet of each other. I have absolutely no worry on that point." She winked, as she fingered her black pearl necklace. "I'll be wearing this necklace or its' equivalent. It's going wherever I'm going." Her eyes sparkled at the fantasy like picture they were formulating. She too thought how easily their thoughts and ideas meshed.

Was any of this possible? It was a high odds gamble. To Rick and Lisa it was the only sensible choice. They agreed. There was no other acceptable way. It had to be done this way. Was there any chance whatsoever of achieving success? It had the same chance as any other adventure, whether it was mountain climbing, trekking across a continent or embarking on a space mission. To achieve their goal there had to try. In agreeing to a plan, they had taken the another important step towards their goal

Their enthusiastic and animated conversation ended when a booming voice behind them shattered the moment.

"Hi Lisa."

Lisa did not have to look up. A chill ran up her spine. She recognized the voice. It was her husband, Eric.

CHAPTER 12

Rick turned to face Eric. He was expecting to see a stern faced, irate husband. To his surprise he saw a jovial, green eyed, red turning gray haired, six foot two hundred thirty pound Swede.

Lisa after regaining her composure stood up and greeted Eric with a hug and a peck on the cheek. She half turned to Rick, "Rick this is my husband, Eric." She stepped back to enable them to shake hands.

Eric reached out his bear paw like hand and firmly grasped Rick's and shook it with a deliberate tight grip. His firm handshake conveyed everything there was to say. "I'm pleased to meet you Rick." Seeing Rick was slightly intimated, he added, "thanks for looking after the little woman here." He laughed at his comment. He patted Lisa on the shoulder and grinned at both Rick and Lisa.

Eric showed no signs of jealousy or irritation whatsoever. He was a self-confident, self-made man. He met and dealt with situations as he found them. "You both wait here. I'll get myself a rum and coke. Do either of you wish anything?" he offered.

"I'll have another red wine, dear." Lisa answered in a subdued voice. She still seemed bewildered at her husband's sudden appearance. Rick declined the offer of a drink. Eric strolled over to the bar.

Rick almost whispered to Lisa. "Do you think I should leave?" he suggested.

Lisa shook her head to show a definite no. "Stay awhile I want you to get to know Eric." It was clear from her voice that she was intensely proud of the respect Eric garnered. He shook hands with welcoming friends in the bar. "Eric will be here until the place closes," she commented. Lisa was happy to have her man back. She reminded herself about questions she had for him when they returned home.

Eric returned and put down three drinks on the table. "Here we go," he said as he put a glass of wine in front of Rick.

Lisa reacted. "Dear, Rick was not having another drink."

Eric looked bewildered "I'm sorry. Gee, how did I mix that up?" he regained his composure and smiled. "And I haven't even had a sip of rum yet."

Lisa and Rick exchanged glances. Lisa commented, "Its o.k. Eric one of our other friends can have it."

Eric settled his huge frame in the chair, resting one elbow on the table. He stared at Lisa from head to foot. "Well look at you Honey Bunch, you're prettier every time I see you." He grinned at Lisa.

Lisa melted at the compliment. "Do you say that to all the women you meet?" She replied in a half-joking, half-accusatory voice.

"Only you my girl," he replied with a smile. He reached out to her chair and with on smooth motion hauled it with her in it right next to his. "I only have eyes for you."

"You sure have a way with words," Lisa blushed. "You should run for politics with all that smooth talk."

"Now that I'm retired, I might.' He looked seriously

at Lisa. "I did tell you, I have taken a retirement package from the company?" He appeared unsure of what he could remember but continued. "They said I may have the early signs of dementia, and should get checked out."

Lisa saw him struggling with the information. "Yes, their e-mail came a while ago. Dementia was not mentioned. I can see why they would keep their opinions to just a verbal statement. Did you ask them to send it?" She gave him a way out of his dilemma. Lisa saw Eric could not remember what he had done.

"Yes, of course. I had the company e-mail you." He gave her a thank you look for the bail out.

Rick saw his opportunity to excuse himself. He stood up and reached out a hand to Eric. "Welcome home Eric, I know Lisa was looking forward to your return. I'm sure you have much to discuss. I wish you a happy retirement."

"Well thank you, Rick. Rick is right isn't it? Have I got the name correct?" Eric again appeared somewhat uncertain.

Lisa interjected again. "Yes, it's Rick, she stood up and gave Rick a small parting hug and whispered, "thank you Rick." She stepped back to let him pass.

Rick had seen the beginning signs of dementia in other people. He hoped, for Lisa's sake that Eric was not going to have to cope with that serious condition.

CHAPTER 13

Lisa was rather concerned as she and Eric drove home the few miles from the Veteran's Club. Eric appeared hesitant as if forgetting which route to follow. He had driven the same way hundreds of times. Lisa hoped it was just tiredness that confused Eric. Having arrived in town after a fourteen-hour flight from London and a one-hour bus ride from Victoria was an explainable reason for his condition.

She would monitor his condition through the night and the next few days to determine how his memory and speech had changed. Now she could see the reason for his not calling her. Was it dementia or exhaustion? Perhaps it was even shame because he was retiring for medical reasons. The precise cause was no longer an issue. She had him back home and she would take care of him. There was no question in her mind about that!

It was seven in the evening as they walked into the kitchen of their house. Puffy, the dog was ecstatic to see Eric. She began tugging on Eric's pant leg. They often played a little game. Eric laughed and put down one bag as he patted her head. She growled and continued pulling on his pant leg. Eric looked more comfortable, now that he was in the familiar surroundings of home.

He carried his luggage to the bedroom, not saying anything as he disappeared down the hallway. Lisa gave him a few minutes and then followed him. As she entered the bedroom, she saw that he had opened the two suitcases and was standing in front of a chest with two drawers pulled out. In his hands he held bundles of clothes in disarray. He was trying to place them into the right drawers. He appeared somewhat confused as to their exact place. Lisa gently reached out to take the clothes from him. "Here Honey, I'll do that for you," she suggested as she stepped forward.

As she began taking the clothes, he reacted. "Get away from me!" He angrily shouted at her and drew his arms to the side so she could not take the clothes away. "I can sort out my own damn clothes. I don't need you to do it." Puffy startled by the commotion, sought safety by hiding under the bed and barking loudly.

Momentarily, Lisa recoiled at Eric's outburst. Then she acted with concern for her husband. She placed her arm around his shoulder and gently encouraged him. "Sit down a moment Eric. I need to talk to you." She got him to sit on the edge of the bed and she had him place the clothes he was holding down beside him. She saw tears forming in his confused eyes as he looked at her. Eric was a proud man. He had just spent thirty-five years captaining ships with crews of some fifty or more men. Now a simple task like deciding on the correct placement of clothes in a drawer sent him into a panic.

"What's wrong with me?" He looked at her with his tear filled blue eyes and took her by both arms as if to steady himself. "I can't remember simple details like I used to."

Lisa sat beside him and held him close. "Tomorrow

we will make an appointment for you to see Doctor Wilson. I'm sure he can help you." She hoped there would be medications or some other treatment that would bring Eric back to his normal self. If Eric became this disoriented during the nine months he was away, she was apprehensive about how he would be in another few months.

She continued to comfort him. "You're just tired, you had a long day. Here, let me help you take your clothes off and get showered. Then I'll fix you a salmon sandwich and you can relax and watch TV." She unbuttoned his shirt, got him to undress, then led him to the shower and started it for him. She stayed with him to see his reactions, which looked normal, even if a bit slow. Lisa brought him some clean pajamas and helped him dry himself and comb his hair. "There you are" she whispered. "Does that feel better?"

He nodded, still in a daze, and he let her lead him back into the bedroom. She pulled back the covers. "You lie here and watch TV while I prepare your sandwich and a cup of tea," she said, turning on a nature show for him to watch.

After a few minutes, she left to prepare the food. She returned fifteen minutes later and found him sleeping soundly, with the remote still in his hand. Puffy had jumped up unto the bed and was lying against Eric's chest with her nose resting on his shoulder. Lisa smiled at the cute picture they presented. She turned off the lights, leaving only a nightstand light on, covered him up and kissed him goodnight. Eric responded with a half smile, as he fell into an even deeper sleep. Puffy was enjoying her place next to Eric.

Rick had arrived home with the rest of the afternoon before him. In one way he was happy for Lisa. She had been hoping for some time that Eric would retire and spend more time with her. Now it seemed to be happening. He hoped the mental confusion Eric displayed was just temporary and that it would subside in a few days.

He decided to phone Meg in Penticton. "How are you?" he asked her as they said their hellos.

"Everything is going just fine. Dad came home today and is right here having an early dinner. Here I'll let you talk to him?" There was a pause as she handed the phone to Karl.

"Hi there Ricky, lad," that was his standard salutation to Rick. He acted like his old self.

"Hi Karl, I hear you're feeling better." Rick was happy to hear the strong tone in Karl's voice

"I'm good for another fifty thousand miles," chuckled Karl. "Come on up and we'll go skiing."

Rick knew Karl was joking. "Perhaps we can go skiing in a couple of months. I am looking forward to seeing you. In fact, I will come up tomorrow. That way, I can spend an extra day."

"That's good news. We'll have time to play cards and talk about our fishing trips." Karl was already reliving their past adventures.

After clarifying the details of his arrival, Rick ended the call. He was looking forward to the drive into the interior of the province.

Rick went about preparing his dinner, His thoughts

turned to Lisa. He decided to e-mail her a short note after he ate. As he went about the kitchen, he thought about how circumstances can change so dramatically in a person's life. What did the future hold for Lisa and Eric? For all that matter, what did the future hold for any of them, including Meg and him?

He sat down at his computer and drafted the message. "Lisa, this is just a short note to let you know we are thinking of you and Eric. I liked him; he seems like a great person. I will be away for a few days. Perhaps we will see you, and Eric, when Meg and I get back. Possibly the four of us, can arrange to have lunch. Cheers, Rick."

CHAPTER 14

Eric was up and stirring at five A.M. Lisa was jarred awake by the clattering of utensils in the kitchen. She hurriedly put on her housecoat and drew it around her as she made her way down the hall. Eric's back was to her. He was lifting a frying pan out of the storage drawer underneath the oven. "What are you doing Eric?" she asked in a low voice, not wanting to startle or upset him.

He turned, as he straightened up and gave her a sheepish grin. "I was going to surprise you and make you breakfast."

I'm glad to see you are back to your old self." Eric had often made her breakfast in the past. Lisa was thrilled that he seemed to be reverting to normal. "Well now, we will see about that!" she exclaimed, as she moved a few steps closer to him.

She took the frying pan out of his hands, placing it on the stove. "Look Eric, you just got home less than eighteen hours ago. It's five in the morning! Come back to bed. I'm sure there are more interesting things to do than fry eggs." Ushering him back into the bedroom, she grabbed Puffy off the bed, put him out in the hallway and closed the door. "Now Eric, you show me where we left off nine months ago. She undid her housecoat and dropped it at the foot of the bed. She climbed into bed and snuggled up against him. Eric's recollection of past events seemed to be intact. He drew her against him and ran his hands down her shoulder, down her back to her smooth warm thighs. Lisa felt all the recent loneliness and the worries melt away. They lost themselves in the pleasures of their early morning reunion. Puffy was whining, to no avail, in the hallway, outside the bedroom door.

෪෪෪

Rick had time to think as he drove to Victoria to take the two hour B.C. Ferries, Coastal Inspiration, over to the mainland. He had a further four hours of driving through the coastal mountain, Coquihalla pass; to reach a point south of Kelowna from there a final forty-five minute drive would land him in Penticton.

As he drove along, he gave further thought to the Reincarnation plan, as discussed with Lisa, Were they just fantasizing and being outright naïve. Was there substance to the plan? He felt serious about the idea and he felt certain Lisa did as well. Was she really tuned into it or merely cooperating? Now that Eric was back with her would she redirect her energies and thoughts to her husband and his dreams? Would she forget about her and Rick's planned future together? Was this all going to fizzle out, just like so much hopeful thinking?

Rick still had this paranormal feeling that there was more than imaginativeness at work here, much more. He had to get some kind of assurance that the theory of Reincarnation had some basis or proof so both he and Lisa could gain the self-assured determination that was necessary to make it happen.

He thought of Meg as he considered the planned situation. Was he being fair to her? Shouldn't he be spending his time engaged in activities and projects in the here and now with her? Should he do that, rather than "day dream" about Lisa and the next life? Was he going to lose his sense of reality by delving too deeply into the future? He had many questions, concerns and desires, but he had no satisfactory answers, to the questions. He had no way to tackle his concerns. He had only yearnings to base his hopes on. "I'm crazy!" he muttered to himself as his car reached the summit of the mountain. He felt the enormity of nature as he drove the high plateau towards Merritt before turning south-west toward Kelowna.

He arrived in Penticton at three p.m., none the wiser, as to his dilemma. He relaxed more as the family reunion took hold. It put him at ease. Here, he could feel he was a part of something real, not imagined. Karl was recovering nicely and had surprised his doctors with his determination to recover quickly. The entire family was bubbling with cheerfulness, as they sat down to a roast beef dinner prepared by Meg and Eva. They complimented each other on the different courses that each had prepared. Apparently, Meg made the greatest gravy on this side of the Atlantic and Eva made the best lemon pie north of Florida. Karl enjoyed the fact he could again be part of the celebrations. It was far better rather than to be wasting away in some sterile hospital bed, getting his nourishment through a tube in his arm. Life for his family was working, as it should. Life was beginning to look good again.

~~~

Lisa and Eric had a leisurely brunch at ten thirty. They had slept in; both were in good spirits, ready to face the day. Lisa took the lead in mentioning about Eric going to see the doctor. She downplayed the reason for her suggestion. "Eric, Honey, don't you think that you should have a medical checkup? It's been almost a year since your last one." She looked genuinely concerned as she intertwined her fingers and rubbed her palms." You showed some signs of forgetfulness yesterday," she said.

Without hesitation, Eric nodded in agreement. "After yesterday's blackout, as you mentioned. I think that you are right. I didn't tell you Lisa, that the reason for my retirement was because I failed the simple medical the company gave me when I got back from my last voyage." He looked slightly embarrassed for not having told Lisa earlier.

"Did they say why there was a problem?" Lisa wanted to get some details.

"All they said, in a roundabout way, was that a few of the crew who had sailed with me before, noticed a change in how I gave orders, and wrote up Company memos. They said I was not always seeing things the right way. You know? I was getting angry at the crew over little things." He laughed. "I thought that was a Captain's prerogative."

"Well then, we will make an appointment with Dr.Wilson. Today is Friday, I will see if he can take you in on Monday morning." With that she picked up the phone and began dialing the number. In less than a minute she turned back to Eric. "The doctor will see you at two on Monday afternoon."

"Thanks Lisa, that will work. Now, I think I will take

a trip down to the garage. My car needs an oil change. I want to say hi to the people over at the curling rink. I may put my name down for this season."

Lisa smiled. She was beaming at the enthusiasm Eric was showing. It was a good sign about him wanting to get back into the mainstream of the town's activities. "I'll prepare us a good home cooked dinner, so be home by five."

He came over and kissed her goodbye. "Oh, I'll be home long before that, probably around two thirty." He put on his seaman's cap and marched out the door, smiling. Lisa could hear him saying good morning to the neighbor next door. She heard them laugh at some joke; she presumed Eric had told a joke. He was always ready with some racy sailor joke or other that he had picked up along his travels.

Lisa's life had taken a 180-degree turn for the better with Eric's return. She hummed a tune, as she prepared the pork roast for the oven.

For a moment, she wondered how Rick was doing. She decided to check her email. She got the meal started and then went into the den. Lisa read the short message from Rick about him being away. She hoped they would see each other during the following week as he suggested. She returned to her kitchen, without replying to the email.

She smiled to herself, as she thought about the plan she had discussed with Rick, for the next life. Even though it seemed somewhat far-fetched, maybe it wasn't complete fantasy, after all. There were numerous reports of people who could recall previous life details and some even began speaking in a language that was completely foreign to them. She would have to look into the possibilities of reincarnation more closely. "Even if they both lived this life, happy with their present status, there was no reason why they shouldn't plan for the next one, was there?"

Thinking further about her true feelings, she concluded that being in love with more than one person was not uncommon. The only unique thing was the way her and Rick were intending to handle the situation.

CHAPTER 15

Rick and Meg began their drive home on crisp fall Monday morning. The early sunlight shimmered off the waters of Lake Okanagan, as they drove northward to the junction of the Coquihalla connector highway. That highway would take them back through the ranch grasslands of Merritt, as they would retrace Rick's route to the Pacific coast.

Meg was content, after seeing her dad in a much-improved condition. She could now focus her energies on Rick and their retirement life in Duncan. She decided to strike up a conversation with him. "Rick, did you water the plants before you left home?"

"Yes, I did, just the way you like it done." Rick appreciated having Meg beside him for the long drive home." I know you will find everything in order," he assured her.

"Did Lisa's husband arrive home? Eric, was his name wasn't it?" She looked closely for Rick's reaction.

"Oh yes, he's home. He portrays quite a commanding figure. He's more than six feet tall, with a big mop of red/gray hair, and hands like small spades. He appears like a guy you don't want to mess with, but he's really very sociable. I met him at the Veteran's on Wednesday." Rick's demeanor brightened as he thought of Lisa.

She raised her right eyebrow; she couldn't help but notice the change in Rick. "Was Lisa with him?" She asked.

Meg's intuition was prompting her to look for more information concerning Lisa.

"Yes, they were there together." Rick thought it better to fudge the truth a bit, rather than go into exact details.

"I'm looking forward to meeting him." Meg again turned and studied Rick's reaction.

He turned to her with a smile. "That's good Meg. I suggested that we might have lunch together some time this week. Perhaps we can do it on Wednesday, before we go to the afternoon social?"

Meg thought for a moment. "That would suit me. I have no commitments on Wednesday," she concluded, then added. "Stop at the tourist rest place on the highway just above Merritt. I want to get some of that local honey."

Rick slowed down as they approached the intersection, and then turned left into the rest stop parking lot. "Once we get the honey, we can slip down into Merritt, for lunch at the Grasslands Hotel." He enjoyed the good food there, along with the friendly service they always provided. He delighted in seeing the local cowboy and logging crowd to whom the hotel catered. It was like stepping back forty years.

The thought "stepping back" made him think in of "stepping ahead" as he again remembered the reincarnation plan he had discussed with Lisa. The more he thought about what seemed like a wild fantasy plan, was now very real and achievable.

Coming back to the present with Meg tugging at his sleeve, he heard Meg's voice. "Rick, slow down! There is the driveway." Rick turned and drove the last remaining yards into the parking area, next to the restaurant. They had a leisurely lunch and drove the short distance back to the highway. Rick was still day dreaming about Lisa. They approached the highway. "Rick, are you O.K.?" Meg said grabbing his arm again, as a logging truck roared by in front of their car. Rick had almost gone through a stop sign.

Meg admonished him. "Rick, are you planning on an early death? If you are then leave me behind, I'm not ready to go yet." She gave him a puzzled look.

Rick smiled inwardly. "If she only knew," he thought. He turned right and accelerated down the highway southwest, toward the town of Hope. Was his subconscious already guiding him towards an early demise? He concentrated on his driving, to take priority over any notion his mind was planning for his future with Lisa.

Meg resumed reading a novel she had started reading in Penticton. Rick was relieved she was starting to relax. He glanced at the cover and asked. "What's that book about Meg?"

"It's called 'A Man a Woman and a Man' written by Liebrecht and Pomerentz. It has a five star rating." She hesitated, and then continued. "The story is about a woman and a man, who meet in a nursing home where they come to visit dying relatives. They soon they fall in love."

Rick was interested. "These people whom they're visiting in the rest home, are they their spouses?"

"They're both visiting dying parents, why should it matter who they are visiting?" Meg looked questioningly at Rick

Rick answered back, as he decelerated for a curve. "I just wondered if the plot would unfold differently, if the persons dying were their spouses."

"It would be a much different story, if that was the plot. Losing a spouse can be far more devastating that loosing a parent. There would be no other thoughts, such as romantic feelings. Don't you think so?" Meg became acutely aware that this discussion with Rick was more than idle chatter. She waited to see what he meant as he responded.

"I suppose you are right, in most instances." Rick did not want to get into semantics about who was more important, a spouse or a parent. "Tell me what has occurred in the story so far?"

"I've just begun the part where they are getting serious feelings for each other."

"I guess the title means she is married?" Rick replied.

"Yes and she has children." Meg replied, again she was having reservations about Rick's interest. "Most women protect their family first. They will even sacrifice their own happiness to achieve that result."

"It sounds as if there are only two possible endings," he concluded. "She either goes with the new guy, or stays with her present husband." He braked, as the car started down a long winding stretch of pavement.

"We'll see. This author probably has more in store for the reader than such a quick, predictable conclusion. I'll let you know." She wondered what Rick was thinking? "Now, how would you script such a story?" Her voice trailed off as if she really did not want him to answer her question.

Rick smiled, as he thought of a plot. "I'm thinking more about futuristic fiction. Maybe the two dying parents, if they are a man and a woman, could be reincarnated and then meet years later and become involved." He glanced at Meg's face, to gauge her reaction. Meg looked surprised at his remark, since it deviated from the novel's plot line. Her face took on a blushed look.

"Why would the people that are dying not reunite with their own spouses?" She asked. "That would be more logical to me, wouldn't you agree?" She closed her book and turned to give Rick her full attention. Meg was not one to allow remarks about relationships go unchallenged.

"Logic has little to do with love." Rick replied. "What I'm saying is that if two people have been in the same nursing home for say, three years and really grew fond of each other would they perhaps hope to meet in the next life?"

Meg snapped at Rick's comment. "That would still be unfair to their own spouses, whether they were still alive or already dead! I still don't see how they could ignore someone who had been their lifelong partner?" Meg was upset at Rick's statements. In her view, what he was suggesting suggested unfaithfulness. To her the wedding vow "until death do us part" was not for interpreting as being a ticket to freedom.

Rick tried again. "We hear of couples, who have been very good friends, where the spouses died and then later the two survivors got together. What I'm describing, is just the reverse. The two deceased partners get together in the future, after the process of reincarnation. In fact, I think it is a cleaner relationship; they both start anew without attachments. They don't have sons, daughters, and friends, all giving them advice on what to do or not to do."

"I understand what you are saying, Rick. You're stating that if it happens here, why can't it happen in the future? I still find it upsetting. I guess no woman wants to lose her husband to another woman, not even in the future." She ended the conversation, by adding, "We have to disagree on that matter!"

Rick was disappointed in Meg's inability to grasp the deeper suggestions in his description of futuristic possibilities. He tried one more time. "We agree that couples find comfort with former friends here all the time, right?" He looked at her.

"Yes that happens. I'm not going to deny that in any way. I for one wouldn't do it." Meg bit her lower lip, trying to remain calm.

"Now take it one step further, what if the deceased spouses of those friends hooked up in the next life? Would anyone care?"

"No of course not Rick, no one here would know!" Meg retorted "The idea still sounds way off the wall to me. It wouldn't work, and I'm tired of talking about it." With that, she opened her book and returned to her reading.

ɤↄɤ

Rick sat there watching the upcoming traffic signs flash by. The approaching traffic came speeding by in an unending stream. They were on the busy artery, between the B.C. mainland and the B.C. interior cities. He wondered if Meg would ever buy into his suggestion that it was a reasonable expectation to move forward into the next life unencumbered. *After all, was it not part of the marriage vows that people were joined together 'until death do you part'? It didn't say forever and ever did it?"* He tried to rationalize their different points of views on the after-life matter. He concluded that it was a woman's nature to think in terms of eternalness, whereas a man thought more in terms of conclusiveness.

$\gamma\gamma\gamma$

After a few minutes Meg closed her book, leaned back and shut her eyes. She began reflecting on what Rick had been saying. '*Was he using this book discussion about future lives as a sounding board on how Meg would feel about such an event happening? It sure seemed <u>like that</u>! If so, was it he who was thinking of having what she would call 'a postdated romance?' If one of the futuristic partners was him, then who was the other future partner? Did he already have one? Was it someone she knew?*' Her eyes opened with sudden realization. "*Oh, my God,*" *she thought.* "*It's that marriage wrecking Lisa. Rick and Lisa have cooked up this disgraceful scheme, to reincarnate and meet in the future.*" She was about to pose that question to Rick, but decided to keep her fears to herself, until she asked a few more discreet questions. In that manner, she could confirm her suppositions, without unduly upsetting anyone. Now that she had in all likelihood guessed the reason for Rick's persistence in pursuing the reincarnation illustration, she knew she was a step ahead of him. She could use that knowledge to her benefit.

$\gamma\gamma\gamma$

Lisa and Eric were entering the doctor's office, for Eric's two o'clock appointment. "Shall I come in with you Eric?" Lisa asked, as they walked up to the reception desk.

Eric agreed. "I think that's a good idea, Lisa, you can explain to the doctor how I keep forgetting details."

They waited the usual fifteen minutes, and then were ushered into a small, windowless examining room. Doctor Wilson had been their family doctor for some fifteen years. He greeted them like neighbors, as he entered the room. "How is Captain and Tennille?" he joked as he shook hands with Eric and nodded to Lisa.

"Tennille is fine but the Captain's boat is sinking," remarked Eric with a jolly laugh.

"What makes you think that, Eric?" Doctor Wilson turned serious, as he opened the file and picked up a pen to make notations.

Lisa decided to speak for Eric. "Eric has been discharged from his job because he was getting irritable and forgetful. During the first day of being home, I noticed he was having memory lapses that are uncommon for him."

The doctor continued to quiz Eric and Lisa about Eric's memory loss. He learned Eric was finding it difficult to do familiar tasks. He was disoriented when driving. The Doctor delved into Eric's poor judgment at work, recent mood changes, and his personality changes. Doctor Wilson got most of the information from Lisa. Eric was somewhat silent, as he realized there were some serious issues with his memory and reactions.

As he was listening to Lisa, Doctor Wilson noticed the red streaks that were very noticeable on her face. He made a mental note to suggest to Lisa that she book an examination for herself in the next few days.

Lisa finished explaining Eric's symptoms. "What do

you think Doctor?" She inquired, anxious to get an encouraging reply.

"Before I say anything further, we had better do a full workup on Eric, including x-rays. Lisa, do you mind waiting out in the office?"

Lisa obliged, by standing up. "Just call me if I can be of any help."

As she turned to leave she touched Eric on the arm. "I'll see you in a few minutes, honey."

Fifteen minutes later Eric emerged from the examining room and came over to Lisa. "I have to go get some blood tests and x-rays." He held up a lab requisition, "and then we have to come back in a week." He had a glum look.

Lisa took him by the arm and steered him toward the receptionist's counter. "Eric Johnson needs an appointment for next Monday."

The receptionist glanced at her computer, stroked a few keys, and then looked up. "Will the same time be O.K.?" She enquired. Just then her intercom buzzed, she took the call and turned to Lisa. "Mrs. Johnson, the doctor has just told me to move up your annual checkup. He's sending out a lab requisition for you as well. He wants to schedule you for two o'clock and Eric for two thirty, next Monday. Does that suit you both?"

"Yes those times are good for both of us," replied Lisa in a somewhat surprised voice. They turned and left the office. Lisa looked at the lab form for herself and saw that no fasting was required." We'll go straight to the lab and take care of these tests, before we go home. Are you up to that, Eric?"

"Sure, let's get it over." Eric was not one to delay matters. Getting tasks done had been the cornerstone of his career. He added, "Then, I want to go to the library and get some books on this dementia and that other mind disorder crap."

Lisa helped him out. "You mean Alzheimer's?"

"Yea, how can I have it if I can't even pronounce it?" He chuckled at his own remark.

"Let's wait for the results of your tests, before we start getting worried. Your problems could be something minor." She hoped she was right, but looked forward with trepidation to next Monday. Why would the Doctor move up her annual examination? She always had one near her birthday in mid-December and this was early November. She assumed the Doctor just wanted to keep December clear for his own reasons. She gave no further thought to the change. They set out toward the lab.

Meg had an idea, as she and Rick neared Vancouver. "Rick, honey, let's stay overnight in Richmond. We can then take the ferry home to Victoria in the morning," she suggested. "We could use a little togetherness, after being apart the last few days."

"Sure, that's a good idea! There's isn't anything urgent waiting for us at home," Rick readily agreed. He was no longer accustomed to driving long stretches on dark, fall nights. "Let's see if we can register at the River Rock Casino?" Rick enjoyed the tele-theatre off track horse racing the casino offered. Meg was partial to the excitement of the video gaming machines. They arrived just after dark and entered the welcoming, spacious lobby. It rivaled most world-class casino operations. They arranged a room on the third floor in the two hundred-room facility

As they were taking the elevator to their room, Meg was deep in thought. She had suggested an overnight stay here so she could get Rick to open up to her, about Lisa. She remembered the interaction between the two of them, and had reserved her opinion until she saw how things developed. Now, with this interest shown by Rick in reincarnation, she had an uneasy feeling. She sensed that the relationship between Rick and her was still secure. She was more concerned with the direction that Rick and Lisa's budding friendship might take in the next few months.

As they freshened up she started a dialogue with Rick, getting right to the point. "Tell me Rick, are you still as infatuated with Lisa as you were a week ago?" Meg was changing into an apple green blouse and doing up the buttons. She turned to face him, portraying a worried look on her face.

Rick was slow in answering. "I'm not so sure 'infatuated' is the right word, honey," he replied trying to diffuse her comment. "Sure I find her interesting. Rest assured you have no reason to worry. She and I are not about to run off anytime soon." He looked in the side mirror and combed his graying hair. "We just have some things in common. Haven't you met someone interesting and hit it off right away?"

"Of course, I have, but there was a difference. They were all women," she stressed, then hesitated a moment, before continuing. "I guess I can see what you mean. Men can have women friends without engaging in romantic relationships. Just keep rule in mind; I don't want an embarrassing situation crop up when we have lunch with them." She emphasized her point. "Will you make sure that won't happen?"

"Don't worry, Meg you will like both of them. You'll see they are a happy couple just like us." He winked at her and smiled. "Now let's go and have dinner and try our luck." They drew the drapes on the window, turned on a night lamp and left the room." He put his arm around her as they waited for the elevator. He had to remind himself that this woman beside him was not Lisa.

In the restaurant, they chose a quiet corner table for two and ordered a light meal. Rick had the beef dip special, Meg had a bowl of clam chowder with Italian bread. They sipped red dry wine, as they waited for their order. Meg was still uneasy, "Rick, do you believe that we all have a soul mate?"

Rick had only one obvious reply to make. "You are my soul mate." He hoped that would convince her.

"I mean do you think a person can have more than one soul mate?" She pleaded for a negative answer.

Rick gave her one "Absolutely not, there is only one soul mate for each of us." He knew by her look, she did not believe his quick, terse answer.

"Be serious Rick, give me a true answer." She took a sip of her wine and glanced back up at him.

"I assume that someone can hit it off with more than one person. Yes, I have to admit that the idea of everyone having only a single soul mate is too remote to believe. I guess it's a matter as degree as to what each person wants to believe." He raised his glass "a toast to all our soul mates, wherever they may be." His eyes sparkled as he held up his glass.

"Stop joking, Rick." Was all Meg could reply. They clicked glasses to complete the toast. She seemed to relax somewhat. She had made her point. Now, she knew where Rick stood on the issue. She always felt that she and Rick were close enough to be considered soul mates. Was Lisa his other soul mate? Was that the common thread that was driving them toward each other and in fact, possibly derailing her marriage to Rick?

CHAPTER 16

Rick was quiet as he left Meg on the main casino floor, amidst the flashing video gambling machines. He took the elevator to the second floor, which housed the Race Book tele–theatre. He purchased a racing form for Windsor harness racing. The monitor on the wall indicated that the second race was running in twelve minutes.

He couldn't keep his mind on the past performance entries for each horse. His mind kept going back to his earlier conversations with Meg, about soul mates and the initial discussion about post reincarnation romances. Had Meg figured out why he had brought up the subject of reincarnation and why he insisted on talking at length about it? Was his relationship with her deteriorating because of his growing obsession with Lisa? Should he shelve the whole scheme of connecting with Lisa in the next life? Was Lisa feeling the same guilt twinges that he was feeling right now? Was all this disruption ruinous to their present relationship with their spouses? Should they declare their love for one another right here, right now and deal with the results?"

On further thought, there were three alternatives. The first, as Rick saw it, was to stay the course and proceed as planned with the reincarnation plan. The second was for them to unite here and now and face the aftermath of that action. The third was to forget being together at any time and just keep living as they were before they met. They could continue their lives as though they meant little to each other. Rick decided those were the three choices, in that order.

He opened the racing form again and began studying it. He had three minutes until post time to make his choice. It was too late to analyze the nine entries in detail. He scanned the names. The number eight horse caught his eye. Its' named was Liz Lover. The driver was Paul McKenzie. Rick hurried up to the wicket and bet ten dollars to place on Liz Lover. The chestnut, a well- conditioned, mare with a blaze of white down its forehead. It started strong in second place, and then fell back to third, halfway around the track. Finally, the horse rallied to finish second, a quarter of a length behind the winner Red Star Hero. Rick was mildly surprised at his good fortune and collected his eighteen-dollar payout.

As he walked away from the cashier's window, he wondered, "If the name similarity was a further sign that Lisa and he were going to be walking down the same path? Why couldn't he stop thinking about Lisa? He was acting like a love struck teenager. Was that it? Was he infatuated, as Meg had said? Would his feelings for Lisa lessen in a month or two?" He wasn't sure what was in store, He just hoped things would work out to everyone's satisfaction. Perhaps he was predicting his own future. Was certainty ever going to come to ease his troubled mind?

In disgust he gave up trying to concentrate on the races and went downstairs to find Meg. Being with her might help him calm down and forget all this unrest in his mind about Lisa.

ᚱᚱᚱ

Meg was absentmindedly going through the motions of operating the video game machine. Occasionally, the sound ringing would signal a small win, jolting her back to reality. She couldn't shake the feeling that Rick was increasingly drifting away from her, toward Lisa. "Did she, Meg, have any power left over him? Was this the end of their forty-year marriage? How much pressure could she exert to regain the status she had as Rick's partner and companion? There had to be a solution. Was counseling in order? How could she explain a theory involving reincarnation to a specialist in human behavior? Would he think her unbalanced to bring up such an absurd idea?"

She printed out what remained of her video machine credits and proceeded to the cashier's window. She would go and find Rick and suggest an early quiet, romantic end to their evening. A little togetherness would help deal with her anxiety. She felt a soft touch on her shoulder. She turned to find Rick standing there. "How did you do with the horses?" she smiled, glad to see him beside her.

Rick glanced at the five dollar bill and a few coins in her hand." About the same as you, I couldn't concentrate on the races" he admitted. "I must be tired from the day's driving."

She took a step toward him and looked in the direction of the elevator and then back at him. "Why don't we call it a night down here. I would prefer to spend a quiet hour or two in our room?" She reached out offering him her arm.

He took a step toward her, linking arms with her.

"That's exactly what I had in mind, Meg. Let's do it." With that, he steered her into the elevator and up to their room.

Rick seemed right with the world, as he opened the door with his pass card and they entered the room. "Do you want anything from room service?" he asked before he took a seat.

"How about a carafe of red wine, I could use a glass or two after today." She answered. She hung her jacket in the closet and turned back to face him.

"Wine it is!" Rick placed the order. Then he dimmed the lights and turned on the music channel. It was nine-thirty. They had plenty of time to enjoy the "away from home magic' that the hotel room offered.

෮෮෮

Lisa and Eric spent Monday night at home. Eric was trying to concentrate on an article he was reading in Golf Pro. He would read a page, start a second time and then have to page back to the first page again. Lisa watched him out of the corner of her eye and saw how frustrated he was becoming. He was unable to remember the information he was reading. After ten minutes, Eric flung the magazine down on the coffee table and announced in a loud voice. "I'm going to call it a night." He stood up and started down the hall.

"Good night Eric," was all she could say, before he had disappeared into the bedroom. Lisa glanced at her watch. It was eight o'clock. She went to make a cup of tea. As she stood by the kettle, she thought about the next few months and wondered how Eric's health would be? "Was he going to deteriorate to the stage where he would require twenty-four hour monitoring? Was her future going to be that of a nursemaid to her husband". She had pined for a normal retirement with Eric. Now that she would be with him, she hoped they could enjoy a few good years. If things got worse, would he be reduced to a mere bodily presence, taking up space?

Then Lisa's thoughts turned to her own health. "What had prompted the Doctor to move up her examination?" She looked at her face in the mirror above the sink and saw the red splotches that appeared on both cheeks. Is that what triggered the appointment?

She poured her tea and helped herself to a cookie from the canister. She then went back into the living room to watch a rerun of the 1960 movie' Strangers When We Meet' starring Kirk Douglas and Kim Novak, where two neighbors fall in love and are forced to make a choice between their love and loyalty to their families.

As Lisa watched the movie unfold, she thought of Rick and her. "Would they have to make a similar choice? What would be the outcome? Could they perhaps carry out their futuristic plan?" It appeared like the only logical choice. The last thing Lisa wanted to do was leave Eric, with his mind slipping into neutral. She would have to tell Rick that she was all for being together: however, it would have to be later, much later.

CHAPTER 17

Meg was still worrying about Rick's detached attitude. She felt that throughout their evening together he was possibly playacting, going through the motions. First as he was chatting and later while lovemaking, proceeding as an actor would in a scripted movie. The intense passion that they regularly experienced was definitely lacking. Even as she strove to provide all the passion she could bring, to make him respond, it did not feel the same. Was she imagining that this was a turning point in their relationship? Could this have been the culmination of a gradual decline in his performance and she had not recognized it? Was it that they were seniors and this was a natural result in their relationship, due to aging? Did Rick have some other underlying health problem? She had to sort this all out over the next few days and fix the problem, if there was a problem!

They boarded the ferry to Victoria at ten a.m. Tuesday morning. They strolled around the deck in the crisp, sunny November morning. Meg got an idea. She would see that Rick and she became close friends with the Johnsons. Perhaps after Rick saw Lisa in everyday situations, the excitement and novelty that sparked their friendship would begin to wane. After that there would be no reason to fret. She brought up the subject. "Rick, did you mention the other day that we would be going out to lunch with the Johnsons?" She paused to await his reply.

100

"Yes, I tentatively suggested that to them. I thought Wednesday would be a good day. After a late lunch we could go to the Veteran's for the afternoon dance social."

"We will be home by one this afternoon. I will phone Lisa and confirm the time and place for tomorrow." Meg saw a surprised look on Rick's face.

"Sure Honey, that would be great," he agreed, still having the inquisitive look on his face

Rick stayed on the promenade deck of the ferry. Meg decided to step inside and continue reading her romance novel. He wondered about Meg's move to begin an outing with the Johnsons. What was that all about? Did she sense that last night he had problems while concentrating his efforts on their lovemaking? He remembered that his mind kept dwelling on Lisa even as Meh was wrapping her arms around him. It would be reasonable to assume that a partner would sense hesitation like that. When he saw Lisa on Wednesday, could he be able to curb his enthusiasm? Would Meg would still be comfortable? How would Eric and Meg react to each other? Rick could see that it would be an interesting lunch. He would insure that it did not become a stressful event for Meg.

Arriving home they had sandwiches and tea. Just after one thirty Meg looked up Lisa's phone number and made the call. "Hi Lisa, this is Meg. How are you this afternoon?"

Lisa took a moment to make the connection. "I am fine Meg. I gather you and Rick just got back. He told me he was going to meet you."

Meg got right to the point. "Yes, we are back and as always, it's a relief to be home. Now Rick suggested that all four of us might go to lunch tomorrow. Are you and Eric available? I'm looking forward to meeting Eric." She hesitated briefly, waiting for a reply.

Lisa agreed, "That will be just fine."

"Rick suggested the Best Western Hotel at one. From there we can go on to the social."

"Sure, that sounds fine for lunch. We'll decide on the social after lunch. Eric is still getting used to retirement. We will see if he is in a dancing mood."

"Thanks Lisa, we will see you at one. Call if there is any change." They ended the call. Meg put down the handset and turned toward Rick. "Is Eric not well?" Lisa mentioned something about him, perhaps not wanting to attend the social."

Rick replied. "He has some memory loss problems. I think his doctors are checking him out. I guess we'll know more tomorrow when we see him. I hope it's nothing too serious.'

She came back to the table. "Anyhow, Lisa said they will meet us for lunch." She picked up the plates and cups and walked to the sink.

Rick stood up changed the topic. "Excuse me Meg, I have to meet with our accountant about some tax planning. We have to discuss it and do something before the end of the year."

Meg left tax matters to Rick and just nodded and said, "Sure Honey, I'll see you later then." She gave him a peck on the cheek. Little did Meg know that today would be a day that would surpass her worst nightmare.

CHAPTER 18

Rick left the house. It was a cool, sunny morning. He started walking the twenty minutes to the office building of Mason and Company . As he strolled along he began thinking once again about Lisa. Rick was looking forward to seeing her and Eric the next day. His thoughts kept alternating between the income tax matters he was to discuss with Cliff Mason and his ongoing thoughts about Lisa.

Rick was enjoying the bright afternoon sunshine as he sauntered along. The traffic was almost nonexistent. He was approaching the Shell station, a block before his destination. On impulse, he made a quick stop at the stationary/post office store and then continued down the street.

Rick heard a shouting voice coming from the direction of the service station. He turned his head, just in time to notice a pickup truck speeding down the small slope towards the street entrance. The same entrance he was just crossing. He threw his body to one side to avoid the truck bearing down upon him. In that split second, he realized the vehicle world be striking him. As he was struck hard, everything went black. Rick felt himself spinning along a brightly, lit tunnel, propelled head first with ever increasing momentum. He entered a fog cloud where he no longer felt any sensation of sound, speed, neither light nor time.

Meg was preparing to vacuum the living room rug when she heard sirens down the street. Sirens, both police and ambulance were an almost daily occurrence. She didn't give them a second thought, as she went about her work. Forty-five minutes later, she was putting the vacuum hose away when the doorbell rang. She hurried to the door, thinking that Rick had forgotten to take his keys. That was something he often did when walking downtown. As she approached the door she noticed through the narrow side light window, next to the door, a police car. Her heart skipped a beat. This wasn't good. Had something happened to Rick? She swung opened the door. Two R.C.M. Police stood waiting. The Corporal was Rob; he remembered meeting Meg at the veterans' club. "Mrs. Morrow?" he inquired.

"Yes," Meg could only whisper, but managed to ask. "Yes, what is it? What happened?" She saw the somber look on their faces.

"There's been an accident." Rob replied, as he glanced down at his notes. "Your husband Rick has been taken to the hospital. I am correct, he is your husband?"

"Yes, Rick is my husband," she replied. She stepped back steading herself by hanging onto the doorframe. "How badly is he hurt?" she asked. "May I go see him?"

"We don't have the full details," Rob offered. "We can drive you over to the hospital, Mrs. Morrow. It would be better than you trying to drive."

She nodded slightly. "I'll get my purse and coat." She went to the closet and was back in a few seconds. "Can we hurry? Please." Tears were forming in her eyes.

They arrived at the hospital and Meg was asked to remain in the emergency room waiting area, until someone came for her. The room held a few persons. Some were waiting their turn for treatment. Others were passing time while loved ones were being treated.

Time stood still while she waited." Why had she not gone with him? They would have driven and Rick would be still unharmed." The police had given her sketchy details of the accident. She knew he had been struck by a vehicle, fleeing the service station, after a robbery.

It was two o'clock. Then it was three o'clock. Finally a person in green hospital garb pushed open the emergency room door. He saw Meg and approached her. "Mrs. Morrow, I'm Doctor James, we can talk in here." He took her by the arm and ushered her into a small examining room just off the waiting area. It had a single small desk and three chairs.

Doctor James helped her take a seat. He removed his green head covering and looked at her, as if formulating his choice of words before speaking. "Your husband came in with severe head injuries," he stated. "There is no pleasant way to inform you. We began operating, but it was not possible to save him. His injuries were too great. He died on the operating table." Pausing as if not comfortable with his efforts. "I'm sorry, we couldn't bring him back." He stopped speaking ,watching Meg grasp the impact of the words he had just spoken.

Collapsing in her chair, Meg, heard those words ring over and over. "We couldn't bring him back." Her Rick was gone! Just like that! Within a matter of three hours, her life changed, changed forever. The doctor stood and came over to her. Assisting her to her feet and steading her for a moment, he asked. "Can I get you a sedative, Mrs. Morrow?"

"No, I just need to see him. May I see him?" She sobbed. She envisioned Rick lying still and cold, covered with a white sheet, motionless on a stainless steel operating table.

"I'll take you to see him in just a few minutes; I'll stay with you until then," he softly assured her. Waiting without any further talking, with Meg quietly weeping into a handful of tissue. The doctor sat by the phone, waiting for the call from the administrator in the morgue. They were both startled when the phone rang. The doctor merely lifted the receiver and listened. He nodded and spoke briefly. "Thank you, we'll be there in two minutes." He turned to Meg. "You can go see him now. Come with me." He offered his arm to her as she stood up.

The elevator was only a few feet down a hall, off the waiting room. They rode down one floor and stepped through the opening elevator door. An orderly stood in silence beside a bed that held a sheet covered body. There was a single chair beside the lowered bed. Meg approached the middle of the bed. The doctor nodded to the attendant. He drew the sheet half way back. Meg gasped as she saw Rick. The finality of the moment struck her. She sat down beside the bed, and reached for her husband's warm but lifeless hand. She gazed in reverence at his face. He looked at peace, even though bruised and bloodied. There was a calmness about him that reflected outward, as if he was trying to say to her. "If this is my destiny, let it be so, I am at peace."

The attendant and the doctor, respecting her privacy, left the room. Meg sat there holding Rick's cooling hand and stroking his hair. Gone were Rick's facial expressions, his raised eyebrows were gone. There would be no more animated hand gestures. Those things were now replaced by a motionless shell, emptied of all robustness. Tears ran down her cheeks. She mourned for her husband and friend. Time was meaningless. There was no longer any reason to be concerned with time. She sat there recalling the forty years of life that Rick had shared with her and their three children.

The thought of their children snapped her back to the present. She must tell them of their father's death. She rose from the chair and placed Rick's arm alongside his body, leaned down and kissed his forehead. The attendant reappeared and drew the sheet up and over the body. He helped her to the elevator and asked, "Do you need assistance? I can get someone from upstairs to come down and help you."

"I'll manage thanks," she whispered, as though not wanting to wake Rick. Meg entered the elevator with a bowed head, unable to hold back tears. Pausing a moment and turning to quietly ask the attendant. "What do I have to do now? Do I call the funeral home?"

"Since this was an accident; the coroner needs a few hours to prepare a report. Leave instructions with the clerk at the desk upstairs about the funeral home that you wish to use."

"Thank you." Taking the elevator to the main floor, she and made her way to the desk.

"I'm Mrs. Morrow; I have some papers to sign?"

A young nursing station clerk who reached in a file tray and replied. "I need the name of the funeral home and a signature from you. It authorizes the hospital to release Mr. Morrow's body." She stood up and placed the form in front of Meg.

"The funeral home is the Valley Funeral Home. My husband prearranged everything." Meg began to weep. Holding up her head she began signing the form in front of her. "Could you call me a cab please?" she whispered to the clerk.

"Certainly, it only takes them a minute or two." She hit a speed dial key and ordered the cab. Meg began walking toward the entrance . A taxi driver was approaching driver to escort her to his cab.

Meg arrived home at five in the afternoon. She decided to wait until morning to phone her two daughters and one son. They all lived out of town. Nothing would be gained by calling them that evening.

༄

Lisa and Eric were watching the evening news on their kitchen TV while having dinner. The news of an accident in their city immediately caught their attention. The reporter announced the details of a foiled robbery attempt at the local Shell station and the subsequent hit and run incident that had involved a retired resident of their community. The police were still looking for the driver and the suspect vehicle, a black Ford F150, with an Alberta license plate. Lisa took note, that the unidentified person killed, was a man in his mid-sixties. "I wonder if we knew him?" she mused. Lisa pondered in her mind, which men she knew from her circle of acquaintances that fit the general description given on TV. After a couple of minutes, she gasped and held her right hand against her mouth. Stifling a thought, that was too dreadful to believe "God!" I hope it's not him," she managed to whisper as Rick came to mind.

"What did you say?" Eric had noticed the frightened look on her face.

"I just had a frightening thought that the man they described may have been Rick from the Legion," she replied.

"I'm sure there are many men in the city that fit that description." Eric tried to lesson her concerns. "The odds are against it being him."

She hoped he was correct. "You're right dear. We should wait until the name is released. I'm sure they will be announcing it on the late news." She couldn't shake the premonition she felt that it was Rick. If it was him, should she call Meg and see how she is? If it turned out not to be Rick, then would she be upsetting both families by speculating? Who could she call that might know the details? Lisa looked over at Eric. She remembered he often played golf with the assistant fire chief, Don Parker. Perhaps Don would have more information. "Eric, would you call Don Parker?" she asked. "See if he knows anything about this? He operates the emergency response team."

"Sure I can do that. I haven't talked to him since I got back." Eric picked up the handset and dialed. A few seconds later he began talking. "Don, this is Eric. How are you?" Lisa saw him pause and listen. Then she heard his reply to Don's remarks. "Yeah, I got back about two weeks ago. I've been busy with medical checkups and the like. How about you, how is work going?" He discreetly steered the topic to the day's events. Again Eric listened to Don, and then responded to what Don said. "We saw the report on the news, do we know the guy?"

In a seconds Lisa's fears were confirmed, as she heard Eric repeat, "Rick Morrow? Yeah I just met him a few days ago at the Veterans. What a shame, he seemed like a good sort." Eric glanced at Lisa and saw her shaking. "Listen Don, Lisa needs some help here. I'll have to call you back in a couple of days. We'll arrange something. I'm looking forward to seeing you." Ending the call, he came over and sat beside Lisa. He held her close; he had seen at the Club, that she had admired Rick. He wanted her to know that he understood the pain of losing a friend. In his thirty-five years of sea duty he had seen many short friendships blown out like a candle flame in the breeze.

Lisa curled up as her husband's arm encircled her. There was no longer any need for words. The unthinkable had happened. Lisa was thinking of calling Meg. She would wait until morning, once the official word was out. The grandfather clock in the living room chimed seven times. It would be a long sleepless night. They sat in the kitchen robotically watching the Wheel of Fortune.

CHAPTER 19

Meg found no peace, as she went from room to room in their home. In every room there was some reminder of Rick. In the entranceway his hat hung on the clothes tree, his footwear was resting neatly against the wall. She went to the kitchen. Rick's after lunch cup of tea was sitting there half-drunk. He was in the habit of adding hot water to his cold tea in mid afternoon. His Sudoku puzzle lay on the corner of the table, pages open, and the puzzle uncompleted.

In the living room his Lazy Boy Chair still had its footrest up. A Dick Frances novel lay next to the chair with a bookmark showing Rick had read about three quarters of the novel. Their wedding picture from nineteen seventy, rested on the China cabinet. Remembering, took her back to how she saw the confidence he had exhibited at their wedding church service. He was standing tall and unwavering as the minister read the vows and asking them to repeat them in turn. She, Meg, had been standing there with knees shaking and the bouquet in her left hand shook, right along with her entire frame. Their children's graduation pictures were placed on either side of the wedding picture. Those were happy years as the children graduated, beginning their careers. Rick and she had to reinvent themselves, and adjust to the fact they were now by themselves. Rick's retirement was another period of readjustment for them as they turned sixty.

The bedroom with the bookcase headboard reminded her yet again of Rick, She had wanted to upgrade their bedroom furniture. He agreed to everything except the bookcase headboard. It had to stay and it did. Each year he would spend several hours deciding which titles he could live without and then selected other books to re-place them. It was his after New Year ritual, sorting out those books.

Meg turned on the TV and lay propped up, fully clothed, on the bed. She began to list things to do. Phone the kids. Phone the Funeral Home. Contact the Church Minister. Arrange a reception for the mourners, and see the lawyer and accountant about estate matters. Her mind began racing from one item to the next. *Would this madness end? Why did life throw so many difficulties in one person's path? Where would it finish? When would things be normal again? Normal? There would be nothing close to normal again. Life with Rick was normal. She could not see herself achieving anything close to that again.*

After a few hours she slipped into sleep, exhausted from the tension she had experienced. She lay there mo-tionless one arm extended across the area of the bed that was usually occupied by Rick. He wasn't there; however his presence persisted.

༚༚༚

Lisa lay in her bed beside Eric. She had not slept at all. Rick's death had traumatized her. Eric had kept her com-pany until eleven. Then he had turned away and fell into a deep sleep. She heard him breathing in a normal fashion.

She felt grateful to have her husband beside her. She wondered how Meg was coping with Rick's death. She said a little prayer for both of them.

Lisa briefly thought back to the reincarnation plan with Rick. "Was it going to happen? Was the accident today, that took Rick's life, connected to their discussions? Lisa shuddered. If that was the case, was she in fact, partly responsible for letting it happen? Surely there was no association between the two actions, their plan and his death?" She hoping not, but she was shivering at the thought. Was this the unfolding of the first part of their plan? What would happen next week, next year or five years from now? Would she know in advance, of her own march toward the end of her life here? Would she soon be on a pathway that would pass across Rick's?" She felt somewhat calmed by the fact that the control of that was resting with some other Force. One that guided all worldly things. From sheer mental fatigue, she finally fell asleep.

CHAPTER 20

Wednesday dawned cool and wet over Duncan. Meg stood against her bedroom window and peered out into the gloom. It seemed as if nature was protesting Rick's death by preventing the sunshine to break through the clouds.

She glanced at the horseracing clock above the dresser. Just four short months ago Rick while on a recent visit to Hastings Park in Vancouver ,had purchased it on a whim. She remembered the heated discussion they had about placing it. Rick had wanted to hang it in the living room. Meg would have none of that. They compromised and agreed to hang it on the bedroom wall. She had grown used to it and found it most useful at night. Its' hands glowed in the darkness, making it easy to check the time of night. She would leave it hanging there. This was their room. She would not change anything that would lessen her memory of him.

The clock read eight a.m. That meant it was nine in Calgary where her son lived. She looked up his office number. He worked at the main branch of the Scotia Bank. She carefully dialed the number (403)221-6401 and got the bank's automatic answering system.

"If you know the extension number of the person you are calling enter it now and press star." She entered 2287, a familiar voice answered.

"Mark Morrow, loans manager, how may I help you?" The voice paused waiting for a reply...

Meg took a deep breath before speaking, "Hi Mark, this is your mom," she replied in a serious voice and waited for his response.

He sensed something was amiss. "Hey mom, you sound worried. Is something wrong?" He immediately thought that this would be bad news about his grandfather. He had been aware of the heart attack he had suffered. "Is it granddad?"

"No son, it's not granddad, it's your dad." She struggled to find the right words. There were no easy words for situations like this. There was no way to soften them. What she was about say would hurt him. "I'm sorry to have to tell you this," she sobbed. "Your father had an accident late yesterday and he's dead."

∽∽∽

Mark sat there speechless, his mind swirling. Then he recalled hearing the tail end of a news report yesterday about an accidental death in Duncan. He began talking. "Oh mom, I heard about that, but did not even imagine it involved dad." Like most people, he thought news like this always happen to other people. He took charge of the conversation. "Look mom, I can be out of here by noon. I'll be there with you by four or so." He had another thought. "Do you want me to phone the girls?" referring to his sisters.

"No Mark, I'll call them from here. It is better if I make the call" She added " Listen, I will send someone to meet you at the airport in Victoria. Just call me back when you know the flight number you will be on."

"I'll e-mail you in a few minutes. Then you can print it out and give it to whomever comes."

Meg made the other calls to her daughters. One lived in Toronto, the other in Vancouver. She explained to them that once she had talked to Mark, she would get back to them with details of the funeral. She went to the den and checked for the promised e-mail from Mark. It had arrived. Meg printed out the arrival time and flight, three p.m. on West Jet flight 176. As she was contemplating who to call to do her the favor of picking up her son. Her phone rang. She answered it without checking the display.

"Meg, this is Lisa." She did not stop, but continued. "Eric and I heard of the accident. We are so sorry about Rick. I don't know what to say, it was so sudden." She finally paused long enough to let Meg respond.

"Thanks for calling Lisa. I appreciate your thinking of us." Meg was unable to say anything further and the line went silent.

Lisa broke the silence "Is there anything we can do to help?". .

Meg looked at the e-mail printout in her left hand. " Yes, there is. My son Mark is flying home at three p.m. Would you or Eric be able to meet him?

Lisa repeated the request, as she motioned to Eric. "Pick up your son at the airport? " She saw Eric nod in agreement. "We can arrange that. Give me the time and a description of Mark."

"It's West Jet Flight 176. You will recognize his luggage. It's black with a yellow ribbon tied around the handle. I'll phone him on his cell and let him know to watch for you and Eric." Meg sighed with relief. With that she gave Lisa, Mark's cell phone number as a backup measure. "I really appreciate your help Lisa."

"If there is anything else Meg, call me back, day or night.

⌒⌒⌒

Lisa turned to Eric. "We have to be at the Victoria Airport by three."

"Fine, if we leave in an hour, we will be there well before that. We can grab a bite to eat while we wait." Eric was happy to be again handing some responsibilities. His whole life had been based on scheduling, planning and deciding. With retirement that had vanished. "I will go fill gas in the car and be back in a few minutes. Would you make some tea to go?" He took his jacket and hurried down the stairs to the door, leading into the garage.

"Please be careful, dear." Lisa noticed the change in Eric's mental attitude and was pleasantly surprised at his eagerness to help. She made a mental note to mention this at Eric's next medical appointment. She began to picture how Mark would look. She knew very little about him, other than he was in banking, single and that he lived in Calgary. Would he remind her of Rick? Did he have his father's eyes and hair? She would know soon enough.

She filled the kettle with water and rinsed out the stainless steel Thermos. Eric traveled with a thermos, on all outings more than an hour long.

Flight 176 was on time. Lisa and Eric stood at the edge of the baggage carousel and waited as the passengers entered the area and began surveying the baggage. They noticed a black medium sized bag marked by a yellow ribbon. A man in his thirties, stepped forward and deftly strong-armed the case onto the floor next to the carousel. He then turned, scanning the surrounding crowd. He spotted Lisa waving wildly in his direction. Eric was standing next to her smiling broadly. Mark approached Lisa. She noted that he was somewhat taller than his father, with more hair. He sported the same infectious smile that had been Rick's trademark. Without any concern of being wrong, she stepped forward to greet him. "Mark, I'm Lisa Johnson." She turned sideways. "This is my husband, Eric.

" I'm pleased to meet you Mark." Eric stuck out his bear sized hand and gripped Mark's hand in a firm manner. "Mark, I'm sorry to hear about your dad."

Mark nodded in acknowledgement of the condolences. "Thank you very much for driving down. I didn't want mother on the highway for a few days." Mark smiled appreciatively. They made their way to the exit and the adjacent parking lot.

Lisa insisted that Mark sit up front with Eric. Once they were under way, Mark asked about his dad. "Can you explain how this all happened, the accident I mean?"

Eric replied, "I have a copy of the News Leader here. It gives all the information the police have released so far." He reached down beside the seat and put the newspaper in Mark's out stretched hand.

Mark silently read the quarter page report and to get the details of the accident. He took several minutes to read and reread the article. Lifting his bowed head, he commented. "It appears quite clear that dad had no chance of avoiding that vehicle."

Eric answered, "It could have happened to anyone who was walking past that driveway at the time." He knew that was small comfort but it was all that he could to glean from the news article.

Mark became pensive, as they took the Malahat highway, north to Duncan. Gazing out at the dark, grey waters of the Pacific Ocean and across the Georgia Strait, he recalled the many times his dad had driven him, as a youngster, to sporting events and on shopping trips. Other than the highway was taking him to see his mother, he was finding little joy in today's drive.

Eric glanced over at Mark from time to time. He and Lisa had not had children and he took a special interest in Mark. He understood the feeling of suddenly losing a parent. It had happened to him when his father was lost at sea. Eric had been twenty-two. He remembered that day as though it had been yesterday.

Pulling into the Morrow house driveway , they stopped. Eric put his hand on Mark's shoulder and patting the young man's shoulder, as he undid his seatbelt. "Your mom's waiting to see you son. Go ahead, I'll tend to the luggage."

⁓⁓⁓

Meg phoned the funeral home and made an appointment for ten the next morning. Mark and she would make up a schedule for the next few days' events. There were so many details to work out and sort into chronological order. She would start with the funeral director and then go from there. She finished reviewing her list and then freshened up the room where Mark would sleep. It was patterned after his room from his high school and college days. They had brought all the pictures and mementos with them from back east.

Meg heard a car pull up. She hurried down the steps and out the door , embracing Mark as he met her halfway up the walk. They held each other, drawing comfort from each other's presence. Eric and Lisa stood by without intruding, on the family moment. Meg turned to them. "Come in, I have some tea and coffee brewing." Her sincerity won them over and they walked up the drive. Eric followed with Mark's luggage.

Meg instructed Mark. "Mark, take those bags and put them in your room. I have it all prepared for you."

Eric stepped forward. "Just show me the way; I will carry them for you." Eric happily followed Mark down the hall. As they entered, Eric saw all the mementos that Mark had accumulated from his younger days, as a junior hockey player. "I see you were quite the hockey player," he remarked as he set down the luggage and inspected the various trophies.

"Dad made sure I had every advantage, to get extensive training and experience." Mark had tears in his eyes. "He often took time off work to make sure I had transportation to out of town games and tournaments. I think deep down, he had wished he had an opportunity to play pro sports in his younger days. It was as though he was hoping I could progress further than the junior ranks." Mark wiped tears from his eyes.

Eric saw the struggle, as Mark tried to keep his composure. "I'm sure he was most proud of your accomplishments Mark, and that he enjoyed every minute watching them. Let's rejoin your mother and Lisa. I could use that cup of tea." Eric took Mark by the shoulder and they walked down the hallway to the living room.

Meg was setting down a platter of cake and cookies that a neighbor had brought over earlier. "Here Eric, you and Mark sit here," she motioned to the open side of the table. "Lisa and I can sit at either end." They spent the next hour chatting about all the happenings going on around the city and nearby towns. It all helped Meg and Mark momentarily from dwelling on the real reason that brought them together. It was an all too brief respite, in what was to be a chaotic week.

CHAPTER 21

Rick's celebration of life was being held on Saturday at the Veterans' club. There was a table display with pictures of Rick. Some of him in his younger high school days, in college and then later ones with Meg and the children, as their family grew.

Mark, along with his sisters Nancy and Sherri, welcomed the one hundred or so attendees, including Eric and Lisa. After Mark's brief statement, a short eulogy was read by Rick's former employer. He had had taken time out to fly in from Toronto.

As Lisa stood there listening to the year-by-year description of Rick's life. It dawned on her that he had made an impact on his community, from the time he was a teenager right up to his death. With the eulogy over, everyone began to mix and move throughout the room. Lisa wandered over to the table display and looked more closely at the pictures and mementos there. Rick's junior league hockey sweater was displayed, along with his team picture; the year was 1970 the year they won the Western Canada junior cup. Lisa had mixed feeling as she surveyed the displayed items. In one way, she felt like she was intruding on the family's privacy. On the other hand, she felt drawn closer to her memories of Rick, as she looked at the piercing eyes in his photos.

She turned away and scanned the crowded room for

Eric. She saw him talking to Mark and Don Parker, Eric's golfing partner who had given them the first news of Rick's accident. She walked over to them. "Hello Don, I haven't seen you for some time!" she exclaimed.

"Hi Lisa," he said giving her a quick hug. "I'm like a chameleon; I blend in with my surroundings." He laughed at his comment, and then continued. "I'll have a quick coffee, and then I have to get back to the fire hall."

Mark interjected. "Why don't we all sit down and I'll arrange some refreshments. What would you folks prefer?" he asked, as he turned to Eric and Lisa.

Eric glanced at Lisa, she nodded. "Coffee and one cream would be fine."

"I'll have my usual rum and choke." Eric added, with a smile. "Once a sailor, always a sailor." Mark set off to get the attention of a server. As they waited, Lisa saw Meg at a nearby table chatting to several women. Lisa recognized them as the main members of the women's hospital auxiliary association. Several of them were regulars at the Veterans' Wednesday social. Lisa hoped they would not upset Meg with any of their comments about her and Rick. She admired the way Meg was dealing with the stress and managing to interact with her friends.

Mark returned to the table, followed by a server, carrying their beverages. He sat down opposite Lisa and took his order of tea from the server. "Help yourselves to the snacks." Mark drew their attention to the platters of food that were being placed on each table. As at most functions involving deaths, there was little to discuss. Each person there realized that life was but a fleeting moment in time. It could end far more suddenly than it began.

It certainly did in Rick's case. There was an air of quiet reflection with only minimal conversation. As a result, the celebration gradually wound down, with only a few remaining people. Before they left, Eric and Lisa said a few words to Meg ,and her family. "Let us know if we can help," Eric offered. "By the way, Mark, do you need a lift to the airport?"

"Thanks Eric, perhaps in a few days. I will phone you for sure before I go, whether I need a ride or not. We'll see how mom feels in a couple of days." He put his left arm around his mother and drew her close to him.

Meg gave him a small smile and a slight nod. She saw the same kind characteristics in her son, which had been passed down from Rick. She did not feel alone, with him and his sisters beside her.

Lisa said a mental farewell to Rick, as they passed the table display. Stopping, she stood there for a brief moment. Would she see Rick another time? She hoped she would. Lisa patted the tabletop softly with her left hand whispering softly. "Goodbye Rick, until we meet again."

CHAPTER 22

On Monday morning Eric and Lisa were back in Doctor Wilson's office. A nurse ushered them in to see the waiting Doctor who was studying a file. He glanced up "Good afternoon Lisa and Eric. Have a seat." As Eric sat in front of him, the Doctor began, "How are you feeling Eric?"

Eric grinned and replied, "Much better doctor, thanks to my wife here." He smiled at Lisa. He directed his gaze back to the doctor. "What did the tests show?"

"The tests were fine. I think what you had was due to anxiety caused by your sudden retirement. Judging from your manner today, I think that was the case. We will recheck you in three months."

He looked at Lisa. "As for you Lisa, we have to do a series of allergy tests. There is something indicating a food or chemical allergy. I can refer you to see an allergy specialist in about two weeks. That would be on November 23. Does that work for you? I'll have my nurse confirm that in a day or two."

Lisa was relieved at what appeared to be a minor problem. She nodded. "That sounds fine." She turned to her husband. "Eric, does that fit in with your plans?"

Eric smiled his impish smile "Yes honey, that's fine." He looked away still smiling.

As they left the medical clinic, Lisa had a question. "Eric, why were you smiling in there?

Eric gave her the reason. "I've booked a few days get-away up Island. We are going to Long Beach next week. Don't worry we will be back by the 23rd."

"Oh Eric, how thoughtful of you. I always wanted to go there!" She hugged him and added "Is it at that newer luxury resort?"

"Yes, it's the Wickaninnish Inn. We leave next Thursday," he replied.

Driving home, they chatted about all the activities available at the resort. In spite of the late fall date of their booking it seemed ideal.

. When they arrived home, Lisa saw the answering machine blinking. "I wonder who that was?" she questioned. She quickly checked. The recorder replayed the message. "Hi folks, this is Mark. Say, I'm heading back to Victoria on Wednesday. Can I impose on you Eric, to drive me to the airport? I have to be there by 4 p.m. Mother wants to come along, but I think she is still a bit shaky. I don't think she should drive back alone in the evening." Call me when you get back. Thanks."

Lisa turned to Eric, who had just returned from the washroom. "Mark wants you to drive him to Victoria on Wednesday afternoon, can you do that?"

Eric replied without hesitating. "Please phone him and tell him I'll be there at two thirty. I want to allow extra time in case there is a highway problem."

༄༄༄

Meg was more relaxed as she answered the door on Wednesday afternoon. She was sorry to see Mark leave, but he had to get back to work. Her daughters had left the previous evening. "Hi Eric, come in, we are just about ready."

"It is good to see you Meg; I didn't spend much time talking with you the other day." Eric apologized.

She nodded and smiled. "It was a hectic day for our family. We can talk today on the drive."

Mark came down the stairs with his luggage. "Hi Eric, I'm ready to go." Mark took his jacket from the closet. They made their way out to Eric's car. During the drive Eric and Mark talked back and forth. Mark was intrigued by the life Eric had led as a sea captain and the many stories he had, relating to the operation of the freighters he commanded. Eric took every opportunity to embellish the stories, to the delight and enjoyment of his passengers. They both recognized his exaggerations.

Meg saw Eric and Mark forming a friendship. They bantered back and forth with comments to each other. She took comfort that Mark made friends easily. She felt that Eric's jovial attitude would help Mark cope with the loss of his dad.

Arriving at the airport, Mark had plenty of time to check in and have a coffee with them before he had to board his flight. Once Mark entered the boarding area, Eric and Meg started the drive back to Duncan, in the dusk. They saw Mark's plane lift off, as they reached the highway junction.

"You have a fine son there Meg," Eric said. "You should be real proud of him."

"We are." Meg realized her word "we," was no longer accurate. "I am." She sighed as she corrected herself." He took to you," she added, looking at Eric." You have such a gentle manner about you."

"My men would not call me gentle," he replied. "Yes, I am a teddy bear, everybody likes teddy bears." He laughed, "Especially a two hundred thirty pound one."

"That must be a Guinness world record." Meg smiled broadly at the statement.

They chatted light heartedly, as the next hour passed. Meg arrived home to the realization that though there had been changes in her life, she still had friends. She could draw comfort from their kindness. She made a mental note to have Lisa and Eric to dinner soon, to show her appreciation for their help. "Thanks ever so much Eric, you have been a great help to us, tell Lisa I will be calling her in a few days."

Eric smiled "Meg, anytime you need anything just call us."

After dropping Meg off, Eric arrived home in good spirits. He gained pleasure from being useful. Doing favors like he did today empowered him. "Honey, I'm home," he announced, as he entered the foyer from the garage area.

Lisa appeared at the top of the stairs. "How did everything go?" she asked.

"It's all done, Mark is probably in Calgary by now and Meg is home and in good state of mind." He bound up the stairs and kissed her on the forehead. "Now let's go in the living room and read these brochures on the Wickannish Inn resort." He handed her the brochures. "Here look these over, while I get a wine bottle and glasses."

Lisa sat on the loveseat and began to read the information.

"Located on Vancouver Island, on the magnificently rugged west coast of British Columbia. We are minutes from the picturesque township of Tofino. Wickaninnish Inn and Pointe Restaurant have received some of the world's most prestigious designations and awards by distinguished hospitality rating organizations. They honor the Inn, the restaurant, and the spa and tell the story of the unusual elements that make this natural destination Inn a top travel choice".

Eric came and sat down beside her. "How does it look?" he asked, as he handed her a drink.

She beamed. "The pictures and descriptions are very descriptive. I can't wait to go!" She took a sip and turned other pages for them to view.

Eric watched her." I'm glad I picked this place then," he said. He took a sip of his wine "I was thinking of taking you to Niagara Falls instead."

Lisa appeared startled. Eric noticed her glass shake. "Is there something wrong Lisa?" He inquired.

Lisa regained her composure. "What would make you think of Niagara Falls?"

"It's romantic," he said. "Many young couples meet there and others go there on their honeymoon. Remember we didn't really have a real honeymoon. I was called to work two days after we got married."

"Well that's right, I remember it well! I was the basis for our first argument. That was then and this is now." She elbowed him in the side. "We will make next week our honeymoon getaway." She shifted her body up against his.

Try as she could Lisa could not shake the thought of her conversation with Rick and their clandestine plan, pertaining to Niagara Falls. *Weird* she thought as they put the brochures to one side and cuddled.

ɤɤ

Meg felt abandoned, as she prepared a sandwich and a cup of tea. The house was quiet, not like it had been for the past few weeks. There was no sports channel blaring out the Monday Night Football game play-by-play commentary, no western and country music emanating from the den. There were no phone calls from Rick's friends. Only, long drawn out silence persisted. She turned on the radio to get some relief. A Freddy Fender hit, "Secret Love," was playing.

The six o clock news reported a news item about an earthquake in Indonesia and the related failure of utility plants and other infrastructure.. The report continued for few minutes. Then the radio reverted to country and western music, as though there wasn't a care in the world. Meg found it both upsetting and ironic, how the world carried on, in spite of disasters. Personal losses such as hers' had miniscule effect. It was merely another figure to add to the government's statistical data.

She switched off the radio and returned to the book 'A Man a Woman and a Man', the very book she had started on her trip home with Rick. The novel had resulted in their lengthy discussions concerning couples uniting after reincarnation. At the time she had adamantly opposed the idea. Now with Rick was gone, she thought back to that discussion. Was Rick going to re-appear on earth as another being? Was it his destiny to meet another woman to find happiness? Meg began to see the positive side of such an occurrence.

She no longer felt threatened by the possibility of Rick having another life. It gave her comfort to imagine a whole new life for him, being reborn, growing up, falling in love, marrying, and having a family. She drew consolation from the concept that he might enjoy life again.

CHAPTER 23

Saturday dawned with a yawn. There were no reports of fires, deaths or serious accidents. Everything was as it was the day before, misfortune had taken a holiday. Lisa scanned the morning paper while she waited for Eric to finish showering. She noticed that the Veteran's Club was hosting a trade show, swap meet and psychic fair. They promoted the event with the slogan "Ask a psychic what you need, and then buy it here." She smiled at the advertisement. She had always had a 'ready' ear for psychics. In most cases they provided positive advice to bolster their client's confidence and helped ease their worries. Perhaps it was time to see what they could suggest for her. What was in her future?

Eric appeared behind her and looked over her shoulder. "What are you reading, Honey?" He asked as he kissed her good morning.

"The Veterans are having their swap meet and fortune telling fair today," she replied. "Do you want to go down there for an hour or so?"

"We can do that." Eric replied. "They usually have some golf equipment. As far as future predictions, that is not my favorite subject." He hesitated a moment and added. "I will take what comes, when it comes."

"I would like to see what she says." Lisa smiled at his simple, but realistic expectations of life. "Besides, this is a

Hungarian Gypsy. She is highly touted in her home country."

Eric scoffed. "If she is so popular, what is she doing six thousand miles from home?"

"Sharing her wisdom with us North Americans," Lisa teased back. She was enjoying the disbelief Eric was displaying.

"You go fortune asking Lisa, and I'll go golf equipment shopping." He had decided he would not make any further comments about the fortune-telling prowess of Hungarian gypsies.

The Veterans' hall was buzzing with activity at eleven thirty, as they walked in the front door and paid their token entry fee. There were some forty booths, tables and alcoves along two sides of the hall and another down the middle of the room. Everything was on display, from clothing to motorcycles to cookie cutters, to baked goods.

Eric and Lisa made their way along one side of the room. They listened politely to the sales pitches by the vendors extolling the super effectiveness of their water purifiers and vegetable choppers. Eric was unimpressed. "It's the same vendors as last year," he commented, as he began scanning through some used books.

"I'm sure you will find something new to amuse yourself." Lisa assured him. Oh look! There is Madame Brigit's booth." She discreetly pointed towards the back of the hall where four alcoves were displaying fortune-telling services. Madame Brigit's appeared the most authentic. Liza steered Eric towards it. Several people were waiting their turn at the entrance. They were all women." Are you coming in with me?" she asked Eric.

Eric was turning away and eyeing the sporting goods tables. "I have better things to do." Smiling, he then added. "Go and enjoy your physic reading. I'll meet you in an hour or so over in the lounge."

Lisa made her way to the last remaining seat. The assistant took her name and told her it would be about thirty minutes. All the prospective clients were quietly waiting. Lisa sat there and wondered if she had to ask questions. Would the reader have a way of finding out what she, Lisa was after? Lisa wanted to ask about Rick and their re-incarnation plan. She was uncertain whether she would have the nerve to ask about it outright. Lisa decided to see how the reading progressed before she would divulge her real reason for coming. In about thirty- five minutes, the assistant at the door collected the forty-dollar fee and motioned Lisa to enter the inner room.

Madame Brigit rose, clad in a yellow colored Hawaiian Moo-Moo, decorated with big painted orange flowers, and probably purchased from the nearby thrift store. It barely covered her 180 pounds of undulating fat. Her dirty blonde hair was bunched up over her head. It was tightly wrapped up in a black nylon turban, making her a foot taller than her four foot four frame. Somewhere in the past she had an incisor tooth knocked out, leaving a noticeable gap when she smiled. Some irate customer no doubt, Lisa thought. Her appearance did not impress Lisa. She was not one to give up.

She continued walking forward. "Good morning Lisa, call me Brigit" was her opening salutation. She was a master at putting nervous clients at ease.

Lisa was taken aback at being addressed by name and

then remembered that the assistant, had taken her name when she first arrived. She must have passed it on to Brigit.

༄༄༄

She took a seat on the opposite side of the old worn table-cloth. Sitting on the table was a Hollywood style "crystal ball" that had seen better days. As a backup measure, on the table, there was a deck of cards, worn with ragged edges. All that was missing to complete the scene was an Ouija board

Brigit dimmed the main lights, and then with both chubby hands wrapped around her crystal ball, she started the session. "Now Lisa, how can I be of service to you?" In the dim light, Brigit flashed her toothless smile. Her eyes intently watched every facial expression Lisa displayed, trying to anticipate Lisa's expectations.

"I want a reading covering the next five years," Lisa replied, deciding to hold back any information that Brigit would just rephrase and repeat back.

"Well these ordinary playing cards should get us started." The psychic said, shuffling the cards. "Tell me Lisa, have you ever had a previous card reading?"

"No." Lisa had to admit she had not sat through an actual card reading before.

"Then I'll explain it as we proceed." She placed three cards face down on Lisa's left. 'These three, represent the past" She then placed three more cards in the middle. "These represent the present." She placed the last three cards on the right. "These represent the future."

"We'll start with the past." She turned the first card

135

face up. It was a king of hearts. "There is a good natured, red-haired man in your present; he helped you. He's a man of few words." She added," He's caused you to worry about him in the recent past."

"That sounds like my husband," Lisa said, without hesitating. She again wondered if the assistant had seen Eric with her and conveyed that tidbit to Brigit. How did she know about the lack of communication with Eric? Brigit may indeed have extraordinary powers.

The second card was a jack of hearts. "You had a warm hearted friend, an admirer."

"Had?" Lisa replied, she thought of Rick.

"Yes, in your pas. It could be as recent as yesterday, or weeks, even months ago. He is no longer in your life." She studied Lisa's face closely, as though she was beginning to recognize what information Lisa was really trying to learn.

The third card from the past was a three of spades. When Brigit hesitated, Lisa asked. "What does that mean? What's wrong?"

"A three of spades means someone was affecting your relationship with your husband. There are two indicators to the same matter, in only three cards. I feel there is a strong force at work here." Lisa's face lit up. Brigit was zeroing in on Lisa's area of interest.

Lisa leaned forward, wanting to know more. "What happens now, can you tell?" She wrapped her arms around herself, as though she was feeling a chill.

"We have the present three cards and then the future three cards to go through yet. They may tell us more." She turned over the first of the present cards; it was a Queen of clubs. "Now a dark haired woman will be giving you advice." Lisa could only think of Sheila. *What advice will she give me?* Lisa thought.

The next card was a two of clubs. "This refers to malicious gossip," remarked the fortuneteller. By referring to the previous card it shows that dark haired woman was involved in this; however, maybe as a conduit, to inform you of the gossip." Lisa thought back to the time her and Rick were exceedingly chatty in the lounge, recalling the disapproving heads turning their way.

The third card of the present group was a four of hearts. "Do you know, you will soon be travelling somewhere?"

"We have no long trips planned," Lisa replied.

"It could just be a few days," offered the psychic.

Lisa thought of Long Beach and nodded. "Yes, we are going up Island for a few days."

"Now we move to the future cards." Brigit was showing signs of her own eagerness to find answers to Lisa's six earlier cards. She turned over an ace of spades. Brigit knew this was not good. Trying to lessen the seriousness of the death card, she whispered, "This card indicates misfortune."

᛫᛫᛫

Lisa knew from movies, that the ace of spades referred to death. "Do you mean I'm going to die?"

"Death is in all our futures." Again Brigit softened her answer. "We all die." She quickly reached for the second last card. It was a nine of hearts. Her brows raised in a questioning manner. "This card is the wish card, a dream fulfilled by looking back at the previous cards; it seems incongruous after a card like the ace of spades."

"Would reincarnation be the possible answer?" Lisa startled Brigit with that suggestion.

"Yes, that could be the reason. At the moment the only other circumstance I could think of is a mother dying in childbirth, with the baby surviving. That doesn't apply here, of course."

Lisa was impatient. "Turn the last card."

"The three of clubs" Brigit announced with relief. "This predicts love and happiness, a second chance. It ties into the previous two cards. I think your idea of reincarnation was a good interpretation. Have you been discussing this matter of reincarnation with someone?" she asked.

Lisa not wanting to divulge the real truth answered, "I read a book about it a few weeks ago." She tried to look Brigit directly in the eyes, but then, had to look away before she finished.

Brigit decided not to pursue the obvious lie. Brigit rose and smiled. "I hope you were not upset by the session? Remember circumstances change from time to time. Check with me whenever you wish." Handing Lisa a business card, and extending her hand, she give Lisa an encouraging smile.

"Thank you for the reading Madam Brigit, I will think about the information I have learned."

As Lisa left to meet Eric in the lounge, she was buoyed by what Brigit had confirmed. Reincarnation could be in her future. What should she tell Eric? Should she tell him anything? Perhaps futuristic things should remain there, and not be brought into the present? She went to join Eric.

CHAPTER 24

Eric was swapping tales with his friends, as Lisa entered the lounge and approached their table. Smiling, she came near. He jokingly said, "Hey Lisa, did that Hungarian guru give you tonight's lottery numbers?"

Lisa smirked and answered. "For forty dollars, I can give you my answer." She joked back. She knew some people did not hold fortunetellers in high regard. Lisa was willing to put up with some ribbing about her confidence predictions.

Seeing she was reluctant to join a group of men. Eric suggested, "I saw Sheila here a minute ago. She may be in the kitchen,"

"Thanks honey, I'll find her." Lisa started toward the back as Sheila appeared.

"Would you care for a coffee, Lisa?" Sheila asked.

"Great! I could use one." Sheila nodded to a nearby vacant table. "Have a seat. I'll be right back."

She reappeared with the beverages. "Eric told me you were getting your future read. How did that go?"

"Same old stuff you know. I will meet someone interesting and all kind of general information." Lisa replied downplaying the effect that the reading had on her.

Sheila saw that there was more to it than that. "I have to tell you, that your friendship with Rick a few weeks ago got the rumor mill grinding." Was there anything to that?"

"Just what you saw, it amounted only to a little good natured flirting. That stopped as soon as Eric arrived home." Lisa had a clear conscience on that count.

"I just thought you should know," Sheila replied. "Now honestly, tell me what did Brigit predict?" Sheila leaned forward to get the full gist of what Lisa had to say.

"Oh, she described Eric without seeing him. She predicted our trip to Long Beach. She finished by saying I would be very happy in the future." Lisa omitted the part about the 'misfortune' ace of spades.

"Did you believe it all?" Sheila wanted more details.

"I'm content to wait and find out." Lisa redirected the conversation. "Now, I'll go and get Eric away from his buddies." She stood up.

Sheila took the hint. "Stay there, I'll send him over to you." She walked across the room and whispered in Eric's ear.

He looked over towards Lisa, excused himself from the table and joined Lisa. "Are you ready to leave?" he offered "it's kind of noisy here in the lounge."

"Take me home," she said "I need a little quiet time."

"Did that guru upset you?" Eric said sensing she was distressed.

"Perhaps a smidgen," she admitted, "you know how they say good things and not so good ones, trying to envelop anything that may happen."

Eric resorted to his pat answer to most uncertainties. "The sun will rise tomorrow honey, you can count on that. That's my prediction."

"You're right of course. Nothing has changed has it?" She got up and they left.

As they drove home, Eric tried again to see what had upset Lisa. "What did she tell you that's worrying you?"

"Eric, do you believe in an afterlife?"

"Do you mean heaven and hell?"

"Well, sort of, and whatever else may be waiting for us."

"I believe we make our own heaven or hell, as we live out our lives." He said with finality.

"And when we die, what then?" She prompted him to keep talking.

"That is the end, you didn't see Houdini make it back, did you?

"What if he came back as another person? Maybe he was reincarnated as another person?" she suggested.

"Then it's a different ball game. He's a different person, isn't he?" No one would know who he is. I could be Houdini and you would never know it." He smiled as he lightened up the topic.

Lisa laughed "Well you did disappear a few times over the years and you did reappear. That gives you a pretty good case for being Houdini."

"Shall we stop and get some handcuffs, chains and a chest with locks?" he continued

"Let's skip that part and just pretend you just escaped and came home to me, your wife."

"What was her name?" Eric played along, happy to see Lisa was livening up.

"Wilhemina, I think?" She kissed Eric on the cheek.

"OK Wilhemina we're home." Eric laughed, as he triggered the garage door opener and drove into place.

For a few hours, Lisa was content to enjoy the present. The future would have to wait.

CHAPTER 25

Meg decided to follow through, on the promise to herself, to invite Lisa and Eric for dinner. She wished to show her appreciation for the help they had been to her family. It was Tuesday morning; she would try to arrange the dinner for Wednesday night. She glanced at the kitchen clock. It read ten a.m. She dialed the Johnson's number and got Eric. "Eric? Good morning this is Meg." She paused, and waited for a response.

"Well yes. Hi Meg, it's good to hear from you." Eric chose his words carefully. "Is everything settling down for you?" He gave her a chance to think. "Is there anything further we can do to help you?"

"For now I'm fine. I just phoned to ask if you and Lisa can come over for dinner tomorrow night." She waited for Eric's reply.

Eric turned to Lisa. She had just come in from the garage, where she had been sorting out the recycling materials. "Lisa, I have Meg on the line. Are we free for dinner tomorrow?"

Lisa nodded in agreement.

Eric spoke into the phone. "Yes Meg, we would be happy to come, thank you."

Meg finished, "I'll see you around six then?" They ended the call.

Meg thought about the conversation she had with Rick

about having a meal with the Johnsons. "How quickly matters can change" she mused.

She went into the bedroom and began clearing out Rick's side of the closet. It was a task that she dreaded. Besides his clothes, there were many files, books and other items in the den and garage that had to be cleared. Remembering Eric's offer to help, she thought she would ask him tomorrow. If he would taking some items to the hospital thrift store, that would free her up for other duties... After what seemed like hours, but was actually only two, she had Rick's clothes, shoes, and bathroom items all packed into separate boxes and labeled. She put the boxes inside the empty closet and closed the door.

The emotional strain of the work left her without any appetite. She made a cup of instant coffee and sat at the kitchen table alone. Here I am, she thought, sixty-five years old, no partner, no kids nearby and not even a pet in the house. Other than her volunteer duties at the thrift store she had no other commitments. She had done everything else together with Rick. That was now changing. Here she was in an unfamiliar city, having been here less than three months and virtually alone. Maybe, she thought, she would feel better tomorrow, after spending some time with the Johnsons.

϶϶϶

Lisa and Eric were deciding what clothes to pack for their trip to Long Beach. On the West Coast, it was necessary to allow for changes in weather. The days could change from rain to sun and back to rain, in a matter of hours.

Lisa was looking forward to meeting people from other parts of North America and Europe. The Inn had gained a reputation as the place to enjoy the rugged West Coast near wilderness experience amid lavish hotel amenities. Puffy ran around excitedly at the sight of the suitcases. She thought she would be enjoying a nice long car ride.

Lisa's attentions turned to Meg and how she was coping with the loss of Rick. She wondered how she herself would react to a situation if Eric died suddenly. Early in their marriage, she had been haunted by the thought of him being lost at sea. As ships became bigger and safer with electronic scanning equipment, she grew accustomed to his work and worried less. Lisa wondered how she would feel tomorrow, being in the house that Rick had shared with Meg. She felt apprehensive about the visit; however, she felt drawn to a place that Rick called home.

Eric came into the bedroom and surveyed the separate piles of clothing Lisa had arranged on the bed, prior to packing. "Hey there Lisa, we aren't going on safari; it's only a four day stay!" he exclaimed. Puffy tugged at his pant leg as if saying "start the car and let's go."

"We want to be prepared," Lisa replied, as she opened up his suitcase and began placing his clothes neatly into the case. "Why don't you order up a Domino's pizza, while I finish up here? I don't have time to cook anything. I like the deluxe."

Pizza was Eric's favorite fast food. "I'll phone it in and go pick it up." The store was only a five-minute drive away. He phoned in the order and gathered up his jacket, hat and gloves. "I'll be back in five." Lisa heard him start the car and drive away. A thought struck her, what if Eric has an accident. What if he won't come back. She rushed to the window in time to see the taillights of Eric's car go dim as he turned onto the main road into town. She began to dial his cell phone and then realized how silly she would appear to Eric. He would certainly remind her, that if he could command a freighter with a crew of over thirty men, he was quite capable of picking up a pizza eight blocks from home.

Reality set in. She put down the handset and went into the kitchen to set out some plates and glasses. She got a bottle of Coor's beer from the fridge for Eric, and put the kettle on for her tea. Turning on the noon TV news channel, to calm herself down, she saw that the weather forecaster was predicting sunny and cool weather, no rain. She smiled as she imagined her and Eric enjoying the hot tub on the hotel patio, as they watched the surf come in and crash on the beach.

Eric came up the stairs two at a time. "Let's eat Lisa, I'm starving." He too seemed to be looking forward to their 'honeymoon getaway.'

Puffy put her front paws up on Eric's leg, as he opened the pizza box. She knew a tidbit or two would be coming her way. Pizza was also her favorite food.

CHAPTER 26

Meg had just returned from purchasing wine as the Johnsons drove up. She walked over to them in the drive and spotted Puffy. "Thanks for coming Lisa and Eric. How are you? She did not wait for a reply. "What a cute puppy" she exclaimed, as she saw Puffy bouncing around in the back seat. Puffy went everywhere and impatiently waited in the car, while Lisa and Eric visited or shopped.

Eric replied, "She's four years old and not so entirely cute. She likes to tug on your pant leg."

Lisa had to remind him. "And guess who taught her that trick?" She smiled at Meg as she closed the car door.

"Oh, bring the dog with you. I love dogs." Meg was drawn to the friendly, tail wagging, fluff ball.

"O.K. then," Eric opened the rear car door. Puffy jumped out and ran straight over to Meg.

Lisa chirped in," He likes you; he didn't bite your pant leg." They all laughed, as they walked up the drive. Puffy ran out on the lawn and started sniffing around doggy style. Then charging past Eric and the women, she went straight up the stairs to investigate her new surroundings.

Shuddering upon entering the house, Lisa saw several boxes stacked near the front door. The boxes were marked, men's clothes, men's shoes, and men's hats, a stark reminder of how recently Rick had been using them. A ghostly presence lingered in the foyer; or was it just Lisa's imagination?

Meg led them up to the living room, past family pictures of Rick and his family. Lisa was still extremely uncomfortable. Then she appeared to relax, as the items reminded her of the few enchanted hours she had spent with Rick. She took comfort from the fact that this is where Rick had last been. She again sensed Rick's presence. Looking around the room, she saw the pictures and paintings that Rick and Meg had acquired. Looking at the items, she felt she would have agreed with most of their choices.

She was jolted back to the present, when she heard Meg speaking. "By the way, I have decided to order dinner in. Do you both like Chinese food?" She inquired.

"Chinese is fine," Lisa responded. Eric nodded in agreement.

Meg picked up a takeout menu from the table. Within a few minutes, they had made their choices.

Meg placed the order. "Now let's have some wine." She continued, "Eric, would you mind coming in the kitchen and opening both bottles, one is red the other white. I'll get the glasses." She showed Eric to the kitchen and produced a corkscrew from the kitchen drawer.

Going back into the living room. Meg put on some music. "Do you like Floyd Cramer?" She asked Lisa.

A surprised look appeared on Lisa's face for a moment. She regained her composure. 'Yes, he is one of my favorites; I have several of his CD's."

"Rick found this CD in Penticton when he came up to get me." She pressed the play button and 'Unchained Melody' began playing. Meg commented on the movie 'Ghost' "Wasn't that a great movie, it featured this song?"

"Definitely, that was a terrific movie." Lisa was flattered, that Rick had purchased the Floyd Cramer CD that they had listened to when she had him over for lunch. She was further amazed that this futuristic song was the one that Meg would choose to play. Tears started forming in her eyes. She recalled the lyrics of the song, as it played, *I need your love. Godspeed your love to me.*

Eric walked into the room, with the opened wine bottles. He noticed Lisa's tear-ridden face. "What's wrong Honey?" He looked at Lisa, then at Meg, and then back at Lisa.

Meg answered for them both." I guess this song has a special meaning for both of us." She reached over and advanced the music to "The Rose."

Lisa recalled the words Sheila had whispered to her, the previous week. "I have to tell you that your friendship with Rick a few weeks ago got the rumor mill grinding. Is there anything to that?" Had Meg gotten wind of those conversations? After all, she was Shelia's friend. In a small city like this, even the least bit of flirting, gets discussed and magnified into a full-blown affair. Surely Meg would not have invited them over, if she was upset with Lisa. Lisa relaxed a bit, as she saw Meg was genuinely worrying at her distraught appearance.

"Here have some wine." She held out a half-filled glass of red. Lisa took a sip.

"I'll be fine in a moment" Lisa replied. "I don't know what came over me" she lied. The ensuing silence was interrupted by the ringing doorbell.

"There's the food," Meg announced, as she reached for her purse and went to the door.

148

Eric came over and comforted Lisa. "It's all right Honey." He had guessed the reason for Lisa's tears. He had tolerated a few comments directed towards him at the Veteran's the other morning, about Lisa and Rick. His interpretation of the entire interaction was no more than harmless flirtation. Eric was no angel; he was the last one to begin bringing up the matter of infidelity.

He and Lisa, for good reason, had never discussed his long absences from home and what he did in the various ports he visited.

Meg returned with the food. "Lisa, would you mind removing the lids off the food, while I get different music on." She placed the food on the table beside the several spoons she had laid out earlier.

Lisa stood up "Great, Chinese food always has that mouth watering aroma," she added. She motioned Eric to take a seat.

Meg put on a Nana Mouskouri CD and returned to the table. "Help yourselves folks." They turned their attention to the dinner before them, and of course had to pay some attention to Puffy. Next to pizza, Chinese food was her favorite. Her favorite Chinese dish understandably was the ribs.

"Is Puffy going with you to Long Beach?" asked Meg.

"It looks like she has to go to "Spring Blossom Kennel." Eric replied, as he smiled at the mention of the kennel's name. " The Wickininish Inn doesn't allow pets"

"I'll be glad to take her for a few days," offered Meg. Eric looked at Lisa for an answer.

" Would you Meg? That would be great! I would far rather she stayed with you. Thanks we'll take you up on that." Lisa replied.

"In return, can we help you with anything, before we leave?' Eric asked.

Meg paused a moment, then asked. "Do you have time tomorrow to go through the garage items, and pack away items which I would never use? You know those power tools and golf equipment? Then take everything including those boxes by the front door to the thrift store? Two hours should do it." She smiled apologetically at Eric, as if perhaps imposing on him and his offer to help.

Eric promptly agreed. "I'll be here at nine, Meg. I'll bring Puffy along so she can get used to you and these surroundings." He reached down and gave Puffy another spare rib.

Lisa looked across the table at the unoccupied chair, picturing Rick sitting there. She wondered what Rick would be saying, if he was actually sitting there. She had to hold back her tears for the second time today. She admired Meg's composure and how well she was appearing to be dealing with Rick's death.' Only Love Can Make a Memory" played softly on the stereo as they had their after lunch coffee. Lisa listened carefully to each word, as the melody played. The song comforted her as it encompassed togetherness. Togetherness was what she cherished most.

CHAPTER 27

Meg felt content that the visit by Lisa and Eric had gone rather well. She was somewhat at a loss to explain Lisa's tear filled reaction to the music. It made her think. Was there really something more than she had imagined, to the flirting Lisa and Rick had on the Port Alberni bus trip? Had it developed into more than harmless dallying? Meg recalled that she had been in Penticton for a few days. Rick and Meg were both without partners for those three or four days. Was that enough to ignite romantic feelings between them? Had they taken a serious step in their relationship? Did something happen that she was not aware of? Maybe that meeting at the Veterans' that Rick had mentioned, was not the only time they had spent together? That would certainly explain Lisa's state of mind at dinner.

Meg decided that she would discreetly talk to Eric. Perhaps he had sensed a change in Lisa's attitude during the past few weeks. She would wait for the opportune time to ask him such a question.

❦

Lisa was sitting at the breakfast table. Eric had gone to the market to get some dog food for Puffy's stay with Meg. Lisa was hoping that Meg had dismissed Lisa's emotional reaction at dinner, hoping she had shrugged off the incident by now. Lisa felt tired and decided to catch a bit more sleep while Eric was out.

The doorbell rang. Glancing out the window facing the street, she saw a flower delivery van stopped in front of the house. It was perplexing to Lisa. They were leaving on their trip tomorrow. She assumed the flowers were from Eric. Why would Eric send flowers now? The van read, "Flowers by Carla" That darned Eric, she thought as she made her way down the stairs to the front door. She smiled as she opened the door to a young delivery girl.

"Flowers for Lisa Johnson," she announced and handed Lisa a dozen red roses. Lisa thanked her and turned to retrace her steps to the kitchen. She placed the flowers near the sink and opened the card attached to the flowers. She read it "Until We Meet Again, My Love." was all it said. She instinctively looked over her shoulder, and then remembered that Eric was away helping Meg. Had someone else sent her the flowers? It had to be Eric, playing a prank on her. This was not at all like him. No, she decided, it was not Eric. Who was it then? She decided to call the Flower shop. She knew Irene, the store manager. She would see if Irene could enlighten her. She dialed the number.

"Flowers By Carla, Bev here. How may we help you?" was the standard reply.

"This is Lisa Johnson. Is Irene in please?" Lisa asked. She thought she heard a gasp in the background and then some excited voices. Then there was silence. Someone had covered the mouthpiece of the phone. After thirty seconds, a woman answered.

"Hi Lisa, this is Irene. How are you?"

"Hi Irene, I'm fine. I just had a question for you."

"Was there a problem with the flowers?" Irene occasionally got complaints.

"Not at all, the roses are beautiful. However, there was no name on the card identifying the sender. Can you tell me who ordered them?" there was a long pause before Irene answered.

"No Lisa, I can't, I'm sorry to say." She sounded sincere.

"Why, is that information confidential?" Lisa pressed her for a reason.

"We just don't know. The order arrived in this morning's mail, with the card and forty dollars, asking us to send you a dozen red roses. It was surprising to all of us; the girls down here think it was most romantic, like a scene from a movie"

"Irene, this is not a movie. There must be some clue? Where did the card originate? What was the postmark date? There must be some more information available?"

"Just a minute, I'll check. I have the waste basket right here." Lisa heard the receiver click followed by a rustling noise. Irene was sorting through the waste paper. "Here is the envelope," she whispered, dated two weeks ago and it was mailed locally. It has our post office stamp on it November the 14, 2011, 2 p.m. I have no idea why we didn't get the order sooner."

"Oh my God!" Lisa exclaimed. Then she realized she was on the phone.

"What's wrong Lisa?" Irene noticed Lisa's reaction.

Lisa had regained her wits. "I believe it was Eric, playing a trick on me." She lied again, "Thanks Irene, I'll get back to you if I think of anything else."

Lisa sat in a state of shock at the table. The letter had been posted the same afternoon Rick was struck by the robber driven pickup. Rick must have mailed it at the post office located a half block before the Shell station. She picked up the card and read it once more. "Until We Meet Again, My Love." Now it made sense. It was from Rick. He must have had a premonition about his impending death. She shuddered to think how very little people knew, about certain aspects of life, up to and including death.

Now Lisa was facing the problem of how to explain all this to Eric? He would be arriving home in a few minutes. Should she just destroy the flowers? No she couldn't do that! They were her last connection with Rick. He had been thinking about her. She could lie and say she bought them her self. Eric would not believe that. They were going away why would anyone buy flowers the day before leaving on a four-day weekend? She would have to come up with a better answer than that. She began crying.

"Lisa? Lisa? Are you all right?" Eric was in the room leaning over her." He took her in his arms. What's wrong, Honey?"

Lisa pulled him to her and held him close. "I guess I had been dreaming. "The late morning sun shone through the bedroom window.

CHAPTER 28

Lisa stumbled to the washroom in a confused daze. Her dream had been so vivid that it was frightening. As she freshened up and brushed her hair, she wondered if Eric had any clue what her dream was about. Would he be asking her? What should she say? She decided to spend a few more minutes of quiet time in the washroom to reorganize her thoughts. The dream mystified her; was Rick sending her a telepathic message from the cloud nine? Should she believe any of it? Was there anyway she could respond? The dream appeared to make the likelihood of reincarnation much more achievable. Then, there was the second phase. Where they would be meeting again? Niagara Falls? Was that possible? Had it been done before?

Eric waited in the kitchen. He put the coffee on to brew and began making some toast. He thought about Lisa? Was she suffering from some anxiety disorder? Was there a connection between yesterday's performance at Meg's, and this one today? Should he launch into a discussion about it with Lisa? Should he ignore the incidents, as meaningless? Perhaps he should have a talk with Meg and get an opinion from her. By comparing observations, they may get a clearer understanding of the relationship between Rick and Lisa. He heard Lisa's footsteps walking hesitantly down the hall. She came over to him and pecking him on the cheek. "I'm sorry about this morning, Honey. I had a strange dream."

"Do you want to talk about it?" Eric nonchalantly buttered his toast.

"Not right now, if you don't mind. Maybe we can talk later today, when you get back from Meg's." She poured two cups of coffee and brought them over to the table.

"Sure Honey. I'll leave it up to you. I don't put much stock in dreams. Let me know if I can be of any help." He spread peanut butter on his toast and followed it up with honey.

Lisa deliberately changed the subject. "Feed Puffy, before you take her, would you? I don't want her to make a fuss at Meg's." She walked to the fridge and took out the jug of orange juice and reached in the cupboard for a glass. "I'm glad Meg's looking after Puffy. They seemed to have really taken to one another.

"Who wouldn't like this little girl?" Eric laughed as he reached down to pat Puffy who was busy tugging away on Eric's pant leg. He dragged her over to the lower cupboard and took out the box of dog food. Puffy let go of his pajama bottom and ran over to her dish and began barking impatiently Eric leaned over and filled it. "There you go girl." He said, as Puffy began crunching up the kibble. He looked at his watch "I have to go in a few minutes; I'll go down and empty my trunk, so my things don't get mixed into the thrift store stuff. Put Puffy out in the back yard. I'll get her from there when I'm ready to leave."

156

"Will you be back for lunch?" Lisa inquired as she walked across the room to put the dishes into the dishwasher.

"I'd say by eleven thirty. If you have something to do go ahead. I can make a sandwich if you're not home." He kissed her goodbye. "Don't forget we leave for Long Beach tomorrow."

"It will be good to get away for a few days." Lisa smiled, as he was leaving the room.

~~~

Eric and Puffy arrived at Meg's promptly at nine. Meg opened the door; Puffy greeted her with a short but friendly bark.

Well! good morning to you too." Meg looked down and smiled. Then she looked up at Eric. "Come in Eric, would you like a cup of coffee before you start loading?"

"Since the thrift store doesn't open for half an hour, a coffee would hit the spot." Eric followed Meg up the stairs into the kitchen.

"By the way, how is Lisa this morning?" Meg asked.

"I was going to discuss that with you, Meg. Lisa woke up this morning in tears. She scared the hell out of me. When I got home from the market, she was sleeping. I went to check on her and all of a sudden she started crying in her sleep."

"Could it be a carry over from yesterday?" Meg stared at Eric, as she set down the two cups of coffee. He was hesitating, before answering her.

"I hope you don't get upset Meg, but did you hear anything around the Club about Lisa and Rick? Was there any gossip?"

Meg stared at him and remembered. "Sheila tuned me in to some of the gossip that was making the rounds. But believe me it was just that. Rick might flirt a bit. He did pay extra attention to Lisa on the Oktoberfest trip. I don't believe for a moment that Lisa and he were anything more than friends." Her expression did not reflect her words.

"I suppose friendships can occur without going any further," Eric agreed. "I'm sorry I brought it up. I agree with you, Lisa has been as solid as a rock for years. I had absolutely no reason to mistrust her. Let us forget the whole matter and call it 'puppy love.'

Puffy reacted to the word 'puppy' and tugged on Eric's pant leg. Eric looked at his watch. "I'd better take that first load of boxes downtown," he suggested. " Will you look after the monster here?" He shook Puffy off his leg.

"We will get along just fine.' Meg scooped Puffy up and held her close. Eric began to carry boxes out to the car.

Eric was back in half an hour. "I'll tackle the tools and other items in the garage," He said to Meg. Sorting out some empty boxes, he began filling them with assorted tools and wrenches. "Do you think Mark would want some of these things? There are some expensive tools here and those golf clubs are top of the line."

"He's not handy with tools; however I could ask him about the clubs." Meg replied. "I'll use the portable phone, in case he has a question for you." She went back upstairs to phone Mark.

Eric heard her talking for a time, then saying "Just a

minute, Mark, I'll let you talk to Eric." She appeared at the garage door. "Mark may want the golf equipment" she handed the phone to Eric.

Eric smiled and spoke into the handset, "Hi. Lad. How are you doing?"

"Just fine Eric. Thanks for helping mom out. I appreciate it." he continued "I think I could make use of Dad's golf clubs."

Eric walked over to them "There are some premium clubs here. This driver made by Taylor Made is a $ 300 item, and some of those Ben Hogan clubs are the most up to date ones on the market. You can't go wrong taking them and trying them out. I'll bundle them up and put them on Greyhound."

"Thanks Eric. By the way, look us up if you come to Calgary." Mark finished the call.

Eric turned to Meg. "He wants the clubs. I'll get a crate from the window company and ship them out when I get back from Long Beach. I should be through here in an hour. Is there anything else that you need help with?"

"The only job left is Rick's den. I would prefer you go through the desk and clear out the old papers and other stuff. I found his will and insurance papers, but couldn't make myself stay in there any longer. It was too upsetting, being in his den, alone.

"I'll be happy to sort through the papers. You may have to decide on the importance of some of the papers."

She nodded, "Bring them to me; we can do that at the kitchen table." She left the room.

Eric was running a little late. He phoned Lisa. He left a message on the answering machine. "Hey kid, I'm going to be busy here until well after one. I'll grab something at the drive through." Eric assumed she had gone out for some makeup or other item she needed.

He returned to packing the tools. Later he sat in Rick's den and started emptying the drawers and scrutinizing the various papers. The first right hand drawer was filled with horse racing forms and handicapping books. Those he trashed, except for a few handicapping books, those he put aside for the thrift shop.

The second drawer was filled with bills and old bank statement reports. These he set aside to be shredded. In the last right hand drawer there were some legal papers relating to the house insurance, property taxes and correspondence from life insurance companies. He set these aside for Meg. She would need to pass them on to the estate lawyer.

At the bottom of the drawer was a brown manila envelope. He opened it up and took out a few letter size papers. The first three were stapled together. They were computer printouts of some internet information about reincarnation. Glancing at them, Eric put them in the trash bin. The second was a print out of some emails Rick had received. Eric was about to shred them when he recognized Lisa's email address as the sender. He read the message.

"Hi Rick, thanks for your message. I have a rather brave suggestion. Perhaps request would be a better word to use. I have received a rather confusing e-mail. It was from my husband's company. I need to talk to someone about it, preferably a man. That way I can get an opinion that is not from a woman's view. I would prefer to do this in a private setting. If you are willing to help me out, I am inviting you to lunch on Wednesday say at noon. That gives us almost two hours before the social.

Eric reread the message. It was reasonable, for Lisa to seek a friend's advice. He turned it over and glancing at the second email it was Rick's reply.

"Hi Lisa. Thanks for your email. Yes, I will be happy to listen to your concerns and offer my opinion on them. Keep in mind that I am somewhat biased since I admire your spirit. You may have to discount some of what I may say. I'm looking forward to having lunch with you and enjoying your company. I will see you at noon.

By the way, I have been looking into reincarnation theories, I may sound completely idiotic; however I think that two people who really care for one another, I won't mention any names, could perhaps meet in the next life and become more than friends. We can discuss this on Wednesday, if we have time. Your friend Rick."

Eric who had been leaning back in the upholstered chair leaned forward, bolting upright. Now, he was beginning to see another picture. Reincarnation! He couldn't believe his eyes. Then he remembered the first computer printout concerning reincarnation. Should he go and talk to Meg about these e-mails? Does she really need to know about them? What purpose would it serve to tell her? It may just upset her, with no benefit to anyone. No, the prudent action was to keep this from her, for now. Eric folded the sheets up putting them in his breast jacket pocket.

He found nothing further of any importance and trashed most of it. He packed the Golf Trophies and mementos into a storage box . Then he went to the door and called to Meg "Excuse me Meg, I'm done here."

Meg appeared at the hallway entrance to the kitchen. " Thanks Eric, come have a sandwich and some tea."

Eric came down the hall bringing the legal papers he had found. "Here are a few things your lawyer may need, and some should go into safekeeping." He placed them on the counter. "The papers in the blue box are for shredding," he continued "I also boxed the trophies and plaques. The room is all cleared out."

Thanks Eric. I'm going to move the desk into a corner and turn that room into a third bedroom." She placed a plate of sandwiches on the table motioning Eric to have a seat. Puffy was curled up sleeping soundly in a box that Meg had lined with an old towel.

Eric smiled upon seeing the dog. "Puffy seems to have moved in. I'll be back later, with some of her toys. If you don't mind I'll leave her here now, so we don't have to bother with her in the morning."

Meg agreed, "That's perfect. If she's any trouble over-night, I'll call you before you leave."

They had an enjoyable quiet lunch. Meg was content that the house was now a more relaxing place. Eric was dwelling on the messages inside his jacket pocket. What approach should he take in discussing them with Lisa? Perhaps he should just let matters be and wait until they got back from Long Beach.

Meg gave him a questioning look. He gazed into her medium blue eyes and smiled, "excuse me Meg I was a million miles away for a moment there."

"Believe me, which is the only place to be at times," she

replied, "That's where I should be too." She had to look away, as she thought about Rick and how recently he had sat there across from her.

Eric could only answer with words. He had seen the same look of despair amongst his homesick crewmen. Resorting to his most used phrase. "Meg, I know, the sun will come up tomorrow." He hoped he was right.

An unexplainable, cold sensation streamed through him, as he was driving home a few minutes later. When he arrived home, Lisa was gone. The note she left was brief. "Eric, I'll be home around one. Love, Lisa."

CHAPTER 29

Lisa had still not gotten over her 'dream experience' as she finished packing for the weekend trip. She looked around to assure herself she hadn't forgotten anything. She checked the time. It was eleven. She decided to go for walk to get some air and perhaps get some relief from her anxiety over the morning's happenings. She expected Eric, though patient would want to discuss the incidents relating to her yesterday and that morning. She left him a short note, saying she would be back at one.

She drove a few miles south of the city to the seashore, where she could stroll on the beach. At this time of year, it would be virtually deserted. At the exit, she stopped at a sandwich shop, deciding to have something to eat, before continuing to the beach. The menu up on the wall advertised a wrap consisting of a dozen shrimp, with a side salad. Receiving her take out order, she drove the five minutes to the seashore. Parking her car, she looked out over the serene Pacific Ocean bay, while eating her lunch.

After finishing, she had a drink of tea from her thermos. Then stepping out into the cool November sunshine, she had walked about half a mile. Suddenly, Lisa felt her throat constricting. She had a sudden feeling of uneasiness, along with discomfort in her chest. Thinking it was indigestion, she turned around to make her way back to her car. Her face began to tingle and swell. Her eyes were swelling almost shut. Lisa realized then that she was having an allergic reaction. She dialed 911 and reported her location and symptoms, as accurately as she could. Her voice was a croaking, choking whisper. The call center nurse advised her to lie down, elevate her feet twelve inches higher than her body, keep as warm as possible, and stay calm. It was a toss up whether anyone going into shock could stay calm, Lisa thought as she followed the instructions. She lost track of time and felt herself slipping into unconsciousness.

The sound of the ambulance siren was heard only by the seagulls as the unit was arriving and the medics were rushing to the side of the prostate figure on the shore. Feeling a weak pulse, they injected Lisa with an epinephrine injection. Quickly loading her on a stretcher, they began the fifteen-minute drive back to the hospital.

Eric saw there was a message on the answering service. Pushing the play button, he heard his message about not coming home for lunch. He erased it. The second message blared out, "This is the Cowichan General Hospital with a message for an Eric Johnson please call us at 250-737-2030. We have an urgent message." He was ready to call them when the third message played out. "This is Sheila. Eric I just had a call from the hospital from a nurse I know. Lisa is in a bad way. Their thinking it may be an allergic reaction. I'm going down there now. Come as soon as you can."

Eric rushed out of the house, driving as quickly as safety would permit. Rushing into the emergency room, he saw Sheila in the waiting area. Identifying himself to the receptionist, he asked. "How is my wife Lisa. She was brought in here a short time ago. May I see her?"

"Mr. Johnson, yes your wife is here." The receptionist looked away as she added. "Have a seat in the waiting area. Doctor Wilson will be out to see you shortly."

Eric turned asking Sheila, "Have you heard anything further?"

"I got here ten minutes ago. They won't let me see her; apparently she was unconscious when they brought her in."

Eric sat down, his face wet with perspiration. He had a strained look on his face. He felt helpless, useless and powerless. He began silent praying for Lisa.

Doctor Wilson came out of the inner ward area walking up to Eric. "Mr. Johnson come with me." Turning he held open the door to the emergency area. Eric motioned Sheila, to come with him. The Doctor knew Sheila, and did not object to her presence. Behind closed doors, the Doctor usher them into an examining room for privacy. He had only a brief statement. "Lisa was given an injection to counteract an allergic reaction. It began to work. She regained consciousness for a few minutes. The injection was too much for her heart. She died twenty minutes ago. I'm sorry we could not save her." He hesitated, allowing Eric and Sheila to absorb the impact of his words.

Eric couldn't believe the Doctor's words. "Lisa is gone? You mean she's dead? How could that be? I saw her less than six hours ago." He wiped his brow with the back of one hand. "Did she say anything?"

"She said only five words. *Tell my husband Eric, Good-bye.*" She was very calm and serene."

Shelia put her arm around the upper part of Eric's huge shoulders. Turning to the Doctor, "May we see her?" she asked, helping Eric to his feet.

"For a few minutes, follow me." Doctor Wilson led them down the right side of the room. Pulling back a curtain, he nodded his head, motioning them to come forward to the bedside area. He drew the curtain back closing the perimeter. Then he uncovered Lisa's face and shoulders. Eric gasped as the finality of death overcame him. Sheila turned white. Sorrowfully they sat beside the bed and saying their goodbyes to Lisa.

Doctor Wilson returning with an attendant interrupted them. "I'm sorry for disturbing you folks. We have to move Lisa over to the other wing now." He turned to Eric, "can you be here tomorrow morning to sign the authorizations?"

"Eric, head bowed, nodded agreement and mumbled. "Thanks doctor, I'll be here." He and Sheila left.

"Do you wish to be driven home Eric?" Sheila offered.

"I'll be all right," Eric replied. He looked anything but all right. "It's four in the afternoon. There won't be much traffic." They stopped by her car. He waited until she left. Then he slowly drove home. Home to an empty house.

Sheila decided to call Meg with the news of Lisa's death.

"Oh my, oh my! Meg gasped "How is Eric?"

"Pretty shook up, it's all so sudden. They were leaving on a short trip tomorrow."

"I know. I have Puffy here. I was to look after her, while they were away." Meg glanced down at Puffy, wagging her tail at the mention of her name. "I'll either go over there or call him" she added, as they finished talking.

Meg felt like the world was ending. What were the odds of two deaths within a few days, amongst a small group of people? Was there some external or supernatural force at play here? Who was going to be the next victim? She knew exactly what pain Eric would be feeling right now. She would take the first step in reaching out to him. She could help him, by being there and sharing his grief. She remembered she had a meat loaf in the oven. Checking on it, she put a cup of rice in the cooker. Thirty-five minutes later, she was ringing Eric's doorbell. Puffy was clamoring at her heels to get in the house.

Eric opened the door. "Hello Meg, "greeting her, he stepped aside, so she could enter. "I suppose you heard about Lisa?" His eyes were red.

"Yes, Shelia called me. I'm so sorry Eric; I don't know what to say." She stepped into the foyer. Eric closed the door.

"Come in Meg. I was just making some tea. Puffy ran up to Eric and then turned and began running from one room to another in search of Lisa. Not being able to find her, she lay in her bed, with a sad look on her face. Her animal instincts let her know that Lisa was gone. Eric was becoming distraught after observing the frantic dog. He went over and carrying Puffy bed and all, closer to his chair.

Stepping toward Eric, "I brought over some food I was making for dinner. I thought we could share it, while I sat with you." Meg said, placing the food on the countertop.

"That's kind of you Meg," He went to the counter

pouring the boiling water into the teapot. "Here I'll help you, I know where everything is." He was putting plates on the table and getting the silverware from the drawer, while Meg was unwrapping the food. They ate in silence. Puffy decided to have a little meatloaf.

Both Meg and Eric were drawing strength by being in the same room together. Finally, Eric spoke," It's nice of you to come over, Meg. People need friends at a time like this, thank you."

"I'm glad I came, Eric, no one should be alone. Have you called your relatives yet?" She reminded him.

"We had no children, Lisa and I. Neither of us have any living siblings. Lisa had a sister, Elizabeth in Scotland and but she died some seven years ago, she had one child, Clara. Other than that one niece, whom I saw only once, several years ago, there are no relatives to call. Can you believe, absolutely no one else!" His face saddened. Then he added. "I'll call Clara and a few of our friends tomorrow. I need a few hours to get accustomed to all of this," he said, waving his arm, in a half circle around the near unoccupied room.

Meg felt powerless. What could she do to help? What did the future promise for either of them? She took the teapot and refilled their cups. It would be a long evening. Ushering Eric into the living room, she made him comfortable in his recliner. She sat at the end of the sofa nearest him, close enough to rest her hand gently on his lower arm.

As years went by the critical time came,
to see if Rick and Lisa would unite as planned.
The author has written alternative endings for this novel

❧

ENDING #1 64 YEARS LATER

CHAPTER 30

2075

Dawn broke on a Scottish moor thirty kilometers June 1, east of Aberdeen. Twenty- two year old Marjorie Nichols awakened from a deep sleep. She had just experienced an extremely realistic dream. Marjorie had dreamt that she had travelled to Niagara Falls, Canada where she met her future husband.

The only detail, in the dream, not discernible was his face. When he had turned to greet her, all she saw was a featureless face, no eyes, no hair color, no eyelashes, no smile, no facial appearance at all. That was when she wakened with a start. "What the hell was that all about?" she muttered. Stumbling half asleep, she made her way to the bathroom.

The dream did not fade into her sub-conscious, as most dreams do. She remembered she had been looking at the travel ads the previous night in the "Aberdeen Independent." Advertised in there was a special tour of Eastern Canada, including a week's stay at Niagara Falls, Ontario.

"That's where it came from," she decided, thinking back to the subject matter of that morning's dream. She brushed her red auburn hair and applied makeup to her slightly freckled face. Taking a high liner brow pencil she touched up her eyebrows. Her hazel eyes liked what she saw, as she looked at her reflection in the mirror. She was looking forward to the day. Would it be one of those life changing days that happen to people perhaps once in a lifetime? Would something occur that would guide the wheels of her future wagon along the right path?

Throughout the day, while working, as a nurse, at the local long-term care facility, her mind kept reexamining the dream. The reference to Niagara Falls was dominating her thoughts, as she started her shift.

During her lunch hour, she went to the travel agency that had advertised the tour. It was only a short distance from her place of work. The pigeonhole travel office was crammed between a bank and a liquor store. Staffing the shop was one clerk. She was, reading a McCall's magazine. Springing to her feet at the prospect of making a sale to Marjorie, she put down the magazine and smiled. "Welcome to Travel's Unlimited." She said in a low and lust voice. "I'm Heather, how may I help you?" She said rising from her seat.

"Good afternoon, I'm Marjorie." Unfolding the newspaper page she was carrying in her purse, Marjorie pointed at the torn out ad from the 'Independent'." I read this ad about your Canadian tour; can you give me more information on this trip?"

Heather reached behind her for a brochure. She turned to face Marjorie. "Have a seat," she answered. She unfolded the brochure. "That's a very popular excursion. In fact we have only five tickets left for the June 24 to July 15 tour. The next one isn't until September, for the fall colors in Algonquin Park." She proceeded to show Marjorie the full itinerary of the tour starting in St. John's Newfoundland, proceeding to the Maritimes, Quebec City, Ottawa, and ending in Niagara Falls, Ontario.

Marjorie's pulse quickened at the thought of travelling to Canada. "I do have three weeks of paid vacation for this year." Making up her mind, she continued. "Yes, I will book the Niagara Tour." Marjorie could not remember when she had been so decisive. She felt a compelling need to travel to Niagara Falls. It was, as if this was a necessary undertaking along her life path.

She put her name down for the trip with a keen sense of calm satisfaction. Back at work she advised the pay mistress of her holiday plans. "Sadie, I'm off to Canada for three weeks starting June 22nd."

"When did you decide that?" Sadie appeared surprised. She had been encouraging Marjorie to use up her vacation time. In fact she had mentioned it just a few days earlier.

Marjorie excitedly related the details of her dream. Sadie took a lively interest in how precisely Marjorie seemed to recall each facet of the dream. Marjorie concluded by saying. "Maybe I'll meet Mr. Right in Niagara Falls," she smiled. The more she heard herself talk about the trip, the more it convinced her it was the right decision.

"It should be the trip of a lifetime," Sadie agreed. "If you do meet your Mr. Right, ask him if he has an older unattached brother for me." She laughed at the serious look Marjorie gave her. "You're really into this aren't you?" Sadie concluded.

"It just feels so right." Marjorie smiled and flicked her hair out of her face. "The more I think about it the more excited I am about going." Marjorie beamed as she turned and walked down the hall to begin her duties on the ward. Was this trip to Canada the start of something new and long lasting? The future would hold the answer to that. Had she taken the first step in finding her lifetime partner?

CHAPTER 31

Evening was approaching in Esquimalt, near Victoria British Columbia, as twenty-five year old Les Schwab was finishing his seaman duties on the HMS Calgary, a Royal Canadian Navy frigate. The discharge he had applied for had come through. He had been at sea for seven months and was looking forward to some R & R. He whistled 'Waltzing Matilda' as he briskly walked down the gangplank for the final time. The ship 'Calgary' had just returned from a series of naval exercises in the South Pacific. Australia had been one of their main stops.

Les had arranged a flight home to Ontario, to his parents' farm near Niagara on The Lake. It had been nine months since he had been home. He was looking forward to seeing his civilian friends, especially his fiancée Linda McPherson, a schoolteacher at Niagara Elementary. Linda had sent him an email, saying she had something of importance to discuss with him on his return.

She has wedding plans in mind I bet, thought Les. He felt settling down to shore job was not such a bad idea. Anticipating their meeting, in Australia he had purchased a black pearl necklace. He had purchased them on impulse, after he saw them in the display window of a Sidney jewelry shop. Some strange inner motivation had prompted him to buy them without hesitation. He recalled how they reminded him of someone in his past that wore a similar necklace.

It was a dull rainy day on June 12, as Les stepped down off the plane at the Toronto Airport. Greeting him were his father, Steve and his mother, Gloria. They were both smiling warmly, as he approached them. They had favored his leaving the Navy, hopeful that he would join them in their fruit farm operation. They hoped, perhaps, he could be taking it over entirely within a couple of years.

As they were driving home, Les glanced at his watch. It was two p.m. Linda was working. He would call her that evening and set up a date for the following evening.

He called her cell at 8 p.m. "Hi honey, I'm back," he greeted her voice mail. "I'll pick you up at six tomorrow. We have reservations at the Charles Inn, on Queens Street."

A few minutes later he got a text message back on his cell phone. "Hi Les, I will meet you at the restaurant at six. However I have to prepare for a PTA meeting at eight. I can only see you for no more than forty five minutes." It was a short and not so 'sweet' message.

What's with her? Les thought as he cleared the message. Linda and he had been on the verge of getting married months ago. A crewmember had taken ill, and Les had suddenly been recalled from vacation to go away for seven months. They could have had a quick civil ceremony before he sailed. Linda had insisted on postponing the wedding until after he returned. Les had agreed, though he did not understand fully at that time, the reason for waiting.

The next day just a few minutes after six p.m. Les' was waiting in the restaurant, hoping to find out what Linda had to tell him. He noticed Linda hurriedly entering the restaurant and proceeding toward his table. She had a grim, determined look on her face. She was dressed in her work clothes, indicating she had probably come straight from school. She looked tired and stressed. Les stood. She gave him a peck on the cheek." Hi Les," was her terse comment.

"You look worn out honey. Is something wrong?" Les hugged her, and pulled back her chair. She slumped down head almost bowed.

"I haven't slept much during the last few nights," she answered. Tears formed in her eyes.

"What's happening here?" Les was not a senseless man. He recognized something was worrying Linda.

"I'll come right to the point, Les." Teachers were good at that. Linda took a deep breath, looking him in the eyes "I'm sorry Les. We're through. I've met someone else." Those nine words must have been a world record for a splitting up line, a line, which while clear was devoid of graciousness.

Les was shocked. He was aware that she had something serious to discuss, but breaking up? That was something he had not imagined. "How could this be happening? We are engaged to be married. Who is this someone else?" he managed to ask.

Linda countered, red faced, "You know him. He's Grant Turner, the principal." She averted her eyes blushing as she said Grant's name.

Les was shocked. "Grant? He's a married man."

"Not anymore. His wife learning of our affair divorced him three months ago." She looked away as her voice trailed off. "It just happened Les. I didn't think Grant and I would ever get that involved."

Les wondered if the affair had already been blossoming when he had left. Was that the reason she had postponed their wedding? He decided there was no point in going there. He nodded slightly, and reluctantly generalized his answer to reduce the tension brewing. "I can see Grant has gained control of your heart. You don't have to say anything further. Perhaps our being together was not meant to be in our future."

Les was disappointed as well as shocked. He realized service men had to deal with long absences from home. Being away at sea for months at a time makes people enter into other relationships. He could understand Linda's vulnerability. He was away. Grant was right there near her, day after day, while he Les was thousands of miles away.

Linda got up. "I'm glad you understand Les." She assumed he did. "I'm really sorry Les." She placed the engagement ring softly in his hand, kissed his cheek and with that she disappeared out the door, out of his life. The engagement ring lay on the table where Les had placed it, sparkling away unconcerned, as if it was just another normal day ending. The sun would be coming up tomorrow. Picking up the ring and stuffing it in his pocket, next to the colorfully wrapped black pearl necklace gift, he stood up. He had lost his appetite, he beckoned for the waiter

Les spent the next two weeks working on the family farm, supervising the pickers harvesting the cherry crop. He welcomed the busy workdays, as it give him time to put aside the pain of the sudden breakup with Linda. At dinner one evening his mother had good news for him. "Your cousin Evelyn from Winnipeg will be in town for a few days. She wants to see Niagara Falls. Would you mind showing her around? You and she were always close when you were kids."

"I like Evelyn. Sure it will be great to see her again." Les recalled the tomboy cousin he had hung out with during summer holidays. He had not seen her for more than five years.

❧

July first was a glorious day. There was abundant sunshine, no wind and the tourist season was booming. Les and Evelyn had reservations for the eleven a.m. tour boat "Maid of The Mist III." They arrived at the loading dock about twenty minutes early. Evelyn was bubbling with excitement. This was her first glimpse of the fall. "Aren't they something?" she said, looking out over the falls, and speaking loudly, over the roaring of the falls.

"I never get tired of coming here," Les agreed. "It's so energizing being this close to nature." They had to wait until the boat passengers disembarked.

While they waited, a tour bus pulled up. The forty or so, brightly dressed, passengers unloaded in clamoring to see the world famous "falls." Les and Evelyn were casually watching as the passengers were gathering beside the bus. Greeting the group was a Niagara tourist guide. The tour group lined up to receive passes. The fourth passenger caught Les' attention. She was a red haired, freckle faced, young woman with hazel eyes. By the look on her face she was consciously scanning the surrounding crowd, as if looking for a familiar face.

Perhaps she was meeting someone Les thought, as he kept looking her way to see if her eyes would fixate on anyone.

Approaching them, her eyes met Les', drawing nearer she began to smile. It started with, just a hint of a smile, and then she broke out into a full, infectious grin. Stepping away from her group with the pass in her hand, she and approached Les and Evelyn.

Les was fascinated with her. He smiled back and made room along the railing for her to get a firsthand look at the falls, motioning her to step forward. Taking his offer, she filled the space. Les felt he should start the conversation. "Hi," he said "From where is your group?" He glanced toward the parked bus.

"From Scotland. I'm from Aberdeen" she smiled again, adding. "Are you also on a tour?"

"No, I live here, just half an hour up the road. By the way, my name is Les and this is my cousin Evelyn." Les could not stop from gazing at Marjorie's bright eyed, smiling face.

"Hi. I'm Marjorie; I am pleased to meet you Evelyn." Marjorie turned back to Les. "You look familiar Les, have we met before? I feel like I know you. Have you ever been to Scotland?"

"No, I've been in many places with the navy, but never in Scotland. Maybe we met in a previous life," he joked. They laughed at the outlandish idea.

Why did he say that, she wondered? Marjorie paused

a moment as if seeming to believe the remark. "We may never know, where or when it may have been or if it ever happened." She smiled warmly.

Accompanying Marjorie onto the Maid, with Evelyn in tow, he asked. "How long are you staying in Niagara, Marjorie?"

"We're staying just short of a week." The lineup was stopping. She moved closer to him feeling his thigh brush against hers. She was not pulling away.

"Great, maybe I can show you a few other local sights." Les moved ever so slightly against her touching shoulders. She edged back even closer against him.

"That would be lovely, thank you." She took his arm firmly. The crowd began filing on board the sightseeing vessel. As they were boarding, they were provided with large yellow slickers before being herded onto the sturdy wooden vessel.

The boat headed straight into the base of the falls. It passed almost close enough for them to touch the falls. Spray stung as the water radiated out from the falls. The boat began rocking as the undercurrent lifted it. Rushing water thundered all around the boat. Marjorie was both excited and a bit afraid as some passengers retreated from the falls side to the opposite railing to avoid the direct spray. "What a magnificent adventure!" she chirped and hung onto Les' arm ever tighter. She felt like this was her place to be at that moment. From time to time both Les and Marjorie stole quick glances at each other. After discovering, each other's eyes locking a few times they both laughed, huddling together. Evelyn could see that in addition to the spray there was magic in the air.

With the boat tour over, Marjorie had to rejoin her group. "I'm staying at the Oakes Hotel, on the U.S side, room 1817" she said suggestively. She hugged both Les and Evelyn.

Les seized the opportunity "I'll phone you later this evening "he promised.

"We'll talk then." She turned boarding the bus.

"What a nice woman!" Evelyn remarked, as the bus pulled away.

"You don't have to tell me that Evelyn." Les was smiling, watching intently as the bus merged with the traffic. Seeing Marjorie waving through the side window, he responded with a half salute.

CHAPTER 32

Les and Evelyn arrived back home. Les' mother, Gloria was in the kitchen preparing the evening meal. "Hi kids." Everyone younger than her was a kid. She looked at Evelyn. "Well young lady, what did you think of the Falls?"

Evelyn beamed, recalling the afternoon's outing. "They were spectacular. No one could describe them otherwise. Seeing them up close was breathtaking

"And you Les, did you see anything new?" Gloria was well aware that Les had seen the Falls dozens of times."

Before Les could answer, Evelyn chirped in. "I'll say he did. A lady, some tourist from Scotland practically had him foaming at the mouth." She looked from Gloria to Les.

"Les foaming captivated over a woman? That is completely not like him." Gloria turned to Les. "Is that right, Les? You met someone new?"

Les smiled, "Her name is Marjorie, Mom. She's a nurse of sorts, from Aberdeen." He paused for a moment. "I'm calling her later." His body warmed just at the thought of spending some time with the red headed beauty who had instantaneously captured his attention.

"Well look at that, from the frying pan right into the fire." Gloria was referring to Les' breakup with Linda. She had not been overly fond of Linda, so secretly, she was relieved when she learned of the breakup.

Evelyn added more fuel. "I never saw two people hit it off so fast." She gave Les a playful kick under the table. He snapped out of his daydreaming trance. "You really were drawn to this gal, weren't you?"

"Don't make too much of it, Evelyn." Les said trying to tone down the rhetoric. "One swallow doesn't make a summer." Getting up, Les, winked at Evelyn as he left. "Now since you two have something to gossip about, I will go help dad in the storehouse."

Gloria took the opportunity to pump Evelyn for more information. "Tell me Ev what is this woman like?"

"She's your typical Scottish lassie. What struck me was how two total strangers could connect that quickly. Once they became aware of each other, they had eyes for no one else. I've never saw anything like it."

"Is she that attractive?" Gloria wanted to know.

"Yes, in a country sort of way, she is very wholesome and completely non-pretentious." Evelyn agreed.

Steve was just finishing a meeting with the pickers and selecting the crews for the next morning. He left the group to finish cleaning up before they left. He saw Les approaching. Steve was a person of few words. "Well son, how did Evelyn like the Falls?"

"They blew her away." Les replied

"They do that to everyone who comes to see them. Thanks for taking her," Steve said as he locked a storage room.

"My pleasure Dad, but you should have gone instead. I could have supervised the pickers." Les hung some shoulder straps and bags on the wall hooks.

"I think Evelyn prefers younger company than an old

uncle. Did you see anyone you knew down there who may give her a whirl?"

"Not exactly, but talking of meeting someone, I met this woman from Scotland. It sounds crazy but she sure gives the impression I had known her from somewhere."

"You two really got along, did you? Steve grinned.

"It was uncanny. Dad, how long did you know mother before you knew she was the woman for you?"

"Three years," Steve had to admit. "That was twenty-five years ago though, that was like the Stone Age compared to now- a- days."

"It didn't sound like whirlwind courtship Dad, what prompted you to propose?"

"Oh, your mother decided all that. She said either I should marry her or buzz off."

"Not exactly super romantic was it? What did you do then?" Les grinned

"You're standing there, isn't that romantic enough? He winked. "Do I have to draw you a road map?" Steve laughed. "I must say I never regretted that night, not for one moment."

"I guess I'm not as patient as you. Marjorie and I are seeing each other tomorrow. I have to call her tonight to arrange it."

"Use the phone in the office here," Steve suggested. "It gives you more privacy than in the house." He winked at Les and smiled, then left to walk to the house.

"Good suggestion, thanks Dad." Les picked up the directory and looked up the Oakes Hotel number and dialed it. "Room 1817," he instructed the hotel receptionist.

"Hello Les how are you?" Marjorie answered.

"Hi Marjorie, how did you know it was me?" Les followed up on her comment.

"ESP" she said. She wasn't joking. "Furthermore, you are standing up and facing south." She was right.

"Have you taken ESP lessons?" Les was impressed.

"It's you, I can do anything since I rubbed shoulders with you!" she said. "I've never attempted anything like that." She continued "I can't explain it." She paused then added. "Well, are you going to ask me out?"

"You sound like my mom," Les replied, thinking of the ultimatum his mother had given to his dad.

"Why would you say that? She sounded curious. Les explained his Mother's ultimatum to his Dad.

Marjorie chuckled "Well Les, I'm not ready to issue ultimatums, not today anyhow, maybe tomorrow."

"What time tomorrow would you suggest?" Les replied.

What? She sounded startled by the question.

"Gotch ya!" Les teased. "I meant what time; shall I arrive at your hotel?"

Marjorie recovered, suggesting. "Let me think, the tour bus gets back at five. We are on our own after that." She giggled.

" May I see you around seven? We can have dinner at Remington's, right there near the hotel."

"That sounds scrumptious Les. Remington's menu is in the room here, I'll look it over." she added "Wear your blue blazer, will you?"

Les got into the act" OK if you wear your black pearl necklace."

It was Marjorie's turn to be amazed. "How did you know I have a pearl necklace?"

"It's ESP." Les wasn't going to tell her that he had just purchased one a month earlier in as a present for Linda.

"Let's stop before we scare each other.' She tittered. "I'll see you at seven."

CHAPTER 33

Les looking handsome in his denim jacket, complimented by the open neck red shirt, arrived at the hotel the next evening. He strolled into the lobby.

Marjorie, wanting to surprise him, was exiting the elevator. "When you say seven, you mean seven." She said glancing at the clock in the lobby. She had on, what appeared to be, a newly purchased denim blazer over a white blouse, with black slacks. Gracing her neck was her string of black pearls.

Les nodded approval. "You look great Marjorie." He offered her his left arm and they sauntered over to Remington's. As they entered, he commented on the necklace. "I love that black necklace. Wherever did you get it?"

"My grandmother inherited it years ago. It came from her sister who lived in Canada. Apparently she died quite suddenly from an allergic reaction." Marjorie tossed her hair back to draw attention to the string of pearls she fondling with her left hand.

A question popped into Les' mind. Her remark had triggered his memory. "Where in Canada?" he blurted out.

"Somewhere near Victoria, British Columbia, I think." Marjorie remembered the story of her great aunt's death.

Les raised an eyebrow. "That is bizarre. I had a male family member out there who was killed in an accident during a robbery attempt!"

"Do you think they knew each other?" Marjorie found the subject intriguing

"If they did, that might explain why we are so comfortable with each other," Les replied. They waited for a hostess to seat them. The relaxing western motif atmosphere impressed Marjorie as the hostess greeted them. They were seated at a private, secluded table between the fireplace and the collection of Bronze sculptures portraying the spirit of the old west. Marjorie was impressed at the unique sight. "Wow! Can we take pictures?" was her first utterance.

"Better than that, they have several postcards at the cashier's counter that will give you professional pictures," replied Les as he pulled back her chair.

"Thanks Les," she smiled as he sat down opposite her. Her hazel eyes sparkled even in the dimly lit room. "Do you come here often?"

"At least once, every time I am on leave," Les replied as he adjusted his chair.

The server sporting western wear handed them their menu. "Any drinks to start?"

"We'll decide on our order first," Marjorie suggested.

Les nodded in agreement. He cautioned himself to be careful what he was thinking in case Marjorie read his mind. They opened their menus.

Looking down at her menu, Marjorie noticed an item "I imagine you have a favorite menu item, since you come here regularly. Is it this T-bone Steak?"

Les was pleased she was not able to guess his preference. "I always have the pan fried pickerel. I would suggest you give it a try. You will enjoy it, guaranteed!"

"If you recommend it, I'll have it," answering softly, after reading the menu description

Pan Fried Pickerel - *Served with a lemon caper butter, seasonal vegetables and steamed rice pilaf*

"I suppose white wine is the standard drink?" he mused "Do you prefer dry or medium?"

"Dry please," Marjorie replied as the waitress came over and took their order.

"That's taken care of," Marjorie sighed. "Now let's get back to us, Les. How come a good looking guy like you is still footloose and single?" She winked and smiled.

"Let's say I was hooked and then released, just like a pickerel in the river," forcing a smile and looking away, not wanting to recount all the details of his breakup with Linda. He turned back to look at Marjorie. "How about you?"

"I'm too busy nursing people to get too involved, shift work and all, you know. I suppose my Mr. Right didn't come along. Younger men seem to be avoiding rest homes." She sipped her wine. "Perhaps you will change all that."

"Did you check your horoscope yesterday to see if Mr. Right was coming today?" Les said kidding her.

"Actually, I did," she blushed. "Do you know what it said?"

"No, tell me. By the way, what sign are you?"

"Virgo. And my horoscope today said I should zero in on what I want. What sign are you?"

"Pisces, don't tell me you have a paper with you?" Les glanced at her purse and realized it could not hold anything close to the size of a newspaper.

"No but I see a newspaper stand over there. Let's get

one and read up on yours. It might be fun!" She nodded at a table in the small holding area.

"O.K". Les played along. He always found psychic's readings interesting. Walking over, and picking up the complimentary paper, he turned to the right page and began reading to Marjorie. "Pisces, if you are single, your status could be changing. Artists and creative types will be far more productive in the near future. Tonight, be naughty and charming. Someone from the past will come into your life." He stopped reading abruptly and looked up at Marjorie. "How about that!" he exclaimed. " Although ,I'm stumped about the 'someone from the past' line."

Marjorie had analyzed each word. "I think you should be keen on the last part." She picked up her serviette as the waitress set down their plates. "I wonder about someone from the past, how many years back qualify as 'the past'?"

Les speculated, "Since I'm twenty -five it couldn't be much more than that, could it?"

"It didn't say your past. It just said 'past' Perhaps it was your relatives' past?"

"Then you must be the person from the past." Les chuckled as he raised his wine glass. "A toast to you and your ancestors"

Marjorie was purring as she raised her glass. "To them and to yours as well!" she said, reaching her glass across the table and clicking with Les'.

"Yes, to us all past and present.' Les replied, smiling. He couldn't take his eyes off Marjorie, looking so perfect, like someone from a dream. Marjorie gave the impression of having pleasant thoughts about him as well "Marjorie, did you consider immigrating to Canada?" Les asked, even before he realized he had spoken aloud.

"Yes, I even told my supervisor I may check out job opportunities here" she admitted. "Wouldn't Sadie be surprised if I didn't come back?"

Les was happy that Marjorie was envisaging such a move. He asked again, "Do you have family in Scotland?" He sipped some of his wine.

"My parents and two aunts live there. I have no brothers or sisters." She looked down at the table. She realized immigrating wouldn't be a huge step. "With today's jet travel, moving here wouldn't be that disruptive to the few family members I have in Scotland."

"I would give a dollar or two to see into the future," Les said quietly as he gazed into Marjorie's eyes.

Smiling and laughing, she said, "The future is what you choose to make it." Reaching for her fork she tasted a small bit of the pickerel. "I like the delicate sweetish flavor"

"Now you know why it's my favorite menu item." Les was pleased at how things were developing.

His cell phone rang. Glancing down he read the display. The call display was indicating it was Linda. He turned the phone off. Linda was no longer a priority. Linda could wait. "Sorry for the interruption Marjorie. It wasn't anything important. Where were we?" He said putting his cell phone away.

"We were enjoying this delicious meal!" Marjorie replied. 'This evening will be the highlight of my entire trip."

CHAPTER 34

Les was in good spirits as he drove home from Remington's. Marjorie was still on his mind. She had agreed to meet him the following day, accepting an invitation to have dinner with Les and his family. He would give her a quick tour of the farm beforehand. Les was planning the day's activities.

He thought of Linda's call. Checking his cell calls and messages, he saw there had been two more messages from Linda. "Call me as soon as you can. It's urgent. I have to talk to you Les." Her voice sounded like she was on the verge of tears. Dialing her number, she was quick to answer. "Thanks for calling, Honey," were her warm welcoming words.

Les was silent for a few seconds. "Hi Linda, you wanted to talk to me? What's wrong?" Pausing, Les gave her an opportunity to answer.

"Grant and I broke up." She was sobbing into the phone. Because she was crying; Les guessed as to who had initiated the break up.

"What happened?" Les tried to show mild concern in his voice.

"He and his wife have reconciled." She again broke into sobs.

On impulse, Les scolded her "What did you think would happen?"

Linda shouted back "She divorced him and now they are reconciling. Who would have expected that?"

Les was getting annoyed. "Look Linda, this is life. Two and a half weeks ago you dumped me; now you are phoning me and crying, precisely what do you want?"

"We were engaged to be married." She pleaded. "Doesn't that mean anything to you?"

"Were, is the main word Linda. "I have the ring you returned, right here in my glove compartment. It's going to stay there, until we both give this a couple of days of serious thought."

"What do you mean Les? I thought you loved me? After all, we saw each other for three years."

"That is why I need a few days to sort out my feelings Linda. This is Friday; I'll call you on Monday." He ended the call and slammed the phone down on the seat next to him.

What do women expect from a man? Les swore to himself as he drove the last few miles to the farm. *Why did life keep throwing curve balls across his plate?* He was a person of logic and planning. He liked to start at "A" and take a straight line to "B," that made sense. *Why couldn't Linda get her act together in the first place and be content with him? Why did she fall for the advances of a married man? Did she not know that would only complicate matters for everyone? Why did she want him back when she threw him aside the first day he returned home? Did she deserve even one more minute of his time?*

His thoughts turned to Marjorie. Was she fickle like Linda? She sure didn't appear the sort. He had known her only two days and yet she was already uppermost in his mind. He would see if they continued their 'Soul Mate' journey during the weekend. A few more days would be hardly a true test of their resolve. It might, however give him enough confidence and insight into Marjorie's complete personality. He decided to stop thinking about Linda and give his full attention to Marjorie.

Marjorie was floating on air after she kissed Les goodnight. Taking the elevator up to her room, she was looking forward to spending more time with Les the next day.

Her travel roommate Joyce, looked up from the novel she held in her hand. She was a middle-aged librarian, a confirmed unmarried woman, happy to lose herself in a good fiction novel.

"Well, my dear" she said looking warmheartedly at Marjorie "How was your date?"

"Wait until I tell you. You will not believe me." Marjorie was bubbling with excitement, as she recited the evening's happenings, including the horoscope readings.

Joyce had heard and read about similar situations before. "Coincidences have happened Marjorie," she began and then saw a look of disappointment come over Marjorie's face. She added "Don't let that stop you from following your dream. Some of these holiday romances can work out very well."

"Are you saying some don't?" Marjorie was looking for further encouragement not discouragement.

"When one of the couple is not sincere, the relationship cools down faster than the tour bus' engine after a two hundred mile trip. You have to make sure Les is as passionate as you are. Be certain that he means everything he says." She added. "He may be a slick operator taking advantage of your naivety."

Reacting defensively, Marjorie shot back "There is nothing slick about Les; he is the most down to earth guy you could find. I'm surprised he is not committed to anyone."

Remembering the phone call Les had switched off, she suddenly felt less confident. Did he have a wife or steady girlfriend? Was he being honest with her? Would Les take her home to meet his folks if he was insincere? She satisfied herself that he was what he portrayed. Was he a down-home country guy bewitched by her charms? "I believe you are mistaken about him Joyce." She stated flatly, as she turned marching into the bathroom.

Les was up early the next day supervising the last few days of the cherry picking season.

They opened up the orchard to the 'self-pick' throng of pickers The volume no longer justified the use of hired pickers. He collected the small fee from each and handed out containers to the enthusiastic Saturday crowd. Kids ran around, adults joked, dogs barked and occasionally fought each other, ignoring their owners' threatening shouts. Reaching the limit of fifty people, within an hour, Les displayed the closed sign much to the chagrin of the latecomers.

He had marked some trees close to the house as reserved for owner's use. He wanted Marjorie to experience the thrill of picking fruit. If he was to take over the operation of the fruit farm, his partner should show interest in the farm way of life.

Steve came by "Good morning son. How did your date last night go?" asking, as he tipped his hat back exposing his forehead.

"Just super, Marjorie is a dream come true.' Les paused then continued," by the way I invited her to dinner here tonight."

"Great your mother and I are anxious to meet her, after the buildup Evelyn has given her. We are looking forward to the opportunity."

"Actually dad, Marjorie reminds me of mom in some ways." Les reminded him.

"Then you are on the right track, son. Psychologists say men tend to marry women that remind them of their mother.

"She's a bit more tolerant than mom; do you remember how mom did not like Linda?"

"Speaking of Linda have you heard from her since you two split?"

"She called last night; she wants to get back together." Les looked serious.

"What did you tell her?" Steve paused to get Les' answer.

"I told her I will think about it and get back to her. I was noncommittal."

"Good, you should be. Take your time you're still young." He turned starting for the house. "I'll tell your mother the news. She can expect company tomorrow."

"O.K Dad" Les turned to check out some pickers leaving with several baskets of picked cherries. He transferred their fruit to a cardboard box, collected the fee, and sent them on their way.

As he watched the family consisting of two parents and three kids were excitedly piling into their car with their 'haul.' He wondered if that scene might be him and Marjorie in a few years.

CHAPTER 35

Les called for Marjorie at five p.m. and headed for the farm. Marjorie was nervous about meeting Les' parents. "I hope your parents like me," she said. She was rearranging her hair and checking her make up in the car mirror.

'What's not to like." Les gave her a reassuring smile. "You'll be the hit of the party."

"Party?" She looked questioningly at him.

"Relax, it's only Evelyn and my parents," teased Les, as they arrived. Bingo, the border collie was always the first to greet anyone who stepped out of a car. Today wasn't any different. He ran over with a tennis ball in his mouth and sitting down in front of Marjorie. She was familiar with border collies; every second farm dog in Scotland had border collie strains. "Look out for Bingo" Les cautioned her. "He's tough on panty hose."

"Ah, he's cute." Marjorie bent down patting his heard and taking the ball from Bingo's mouth. He began crouching down with amber eyes focusing on the ball. Marjorie flung the ball some sixty yards. Bingo had it on the first bounce. 'Good boy," she crooned as he rushed back and dropping it at her feet. Les took Marjorie's left arm and escorting her toward the house. Bingo stalked the ball still in Marjorie's hand. Once they were on the steps, she tossed it once more. Bingo responded and was off. They entered the house.

Gloria turned as they came down the hall and into the kitchen, where she was readying some steaks for the barbeque. "Right on time kids." She smiled as she saw Marjorie.

Les stepped forward, "Marjorie, this is my mother Gloria." He turned to face Evelyn, "and you met Evelyn at the Falls."

Marjorie returned the smiles. "Hello Mrs. Schwab." She took a few steps forward and gave Gloria a quick hug. Turning, she continued. 'Lovely to see you again Evelyn."

"Hi Marjorie, how is your vacation going? Come have a seat." She motioned to the chair across from her.

"Just terrific! We were in Toronto today, touring the city. The two hours each way was an exceptionally scenic trip, many different landscapes and developments along the highway."

"Did you see the zoo?" Evelyn asked.

"It was the first stop. I rather enjoyed the polar bears, otters and hippos. Then we went to the Black Creek Pioneer Village. I really enjoyed that 1800's recreated setting. After that we went to see city hall and one of the museums."

Gloria interrupted. "Les would you take theses steaks out to your dad?"

"Sure Mom." Les picked up the platter, heading out the back door to the patio area.

"Quite the son you have there, Mrs. Schwab!" Marjorie exclaimed.

"Thanks Marjorie, he's like his father. Les needs a woman to keep him on the straight and narrow." She winked at Marjorie then continued. "That's why the Navy suited him. He knew exactly what his duties were."

"I understand he is no longer a Navy man?" Marjorie replied.

"He took a bit of a wrong turn there. Les was engaged and returning home to get married and settle down. I'll let him explain it to you in good time." She continued, 'Let's go join the men on the patio." Picking up some salad items, she began walking out to the patio. Evelyn and Marjorie followed with the remaining items.

The steaks were grilling on the barbeque. Bingo, as usual was standing guard to ensure bones would come his way; his eyes were focusing on every move Steve made as he turned the steaks every few minutes.

Les came over. "Try this cherry wine Marjorie. We made it right here on the farm." Producing a fistful of glasses and setting them down on the patio table, he filled them, handing everyone a glass.

Steve came over and got the last one. "A toast to our guest Marjorie and our son, back home to stay." They all agreed and tested the wine.

"Last year" quipped Les, "a very good year." They all laughed.

"I like the smooth, sweet taste," commented Marjorie. "Very pleasant indeed."

The late afternoon was filled with stimulating conversation, good food and some western music from a portable CD player. It was a pleasant July evening with the sun retreating from the patio with the passing minutes.

After the meal, Les suggested that he and Marjorie stroll through the nearby cherry orchard. She could try her hand at picking. As they strolled along Les, saw that Marjorie was enjoying the Canadian lifestyle of space and laid back pace. He broached the question. "Well Marjorie, does this fit in with that dream you said you had?"

She sidestepped the question "It certainly is a lovely area, and your family couldn't be friendlier." She smiled and squeezed Les' hand as they walked along. "Your mother said you may take over the farm?"

"That was the plan when I left the Navy. Now I'm not so sure." Les looked down at the turf.

Marjorie feigned ignorance. "Why do you say that Les?"

"I had a fiancé that broke off our engagement when I returned." He blurted out.

"Oh my, that must have been a shock. What happened?"

"She thought she found someone else."

"Thought?"

"That is over. Now she wants us to resume our relationship. That call in the restaurant was from her," he admitted.

"I noticed that you were distracted by it," Marjorie commented kicking one of Bingo's balls up the path.

"Everything is back where it was then. You should be pleased." She could see Les was having an inner struggle "matters should begin sorting themselves out in time."

"I'll be dealing with all that, in the next couple of days, Marjorie; I think I know what to do." He said handing her a picking basket

Smiling at Les as she took the basket, "Now let's start picking cherries." Seeing a ladder propped up against a tree, she began climbing up filling the basket with cherries. Squeezing up into the middle branches, she continued picking, occasionally popping one in her mouth.

"These are delicious," she said hollering down to Les, steading the ladder.

"I'm glad you are enjoying them. Pick all you want, take some back to the hotel for your group."

"I will, they will love them!" She continued stripping cherries into the basket." What a wonderful day!" she exclaimed, lowering the basket of fruit to Les and then climbing down.

"I agree." Les put one arm around her waist, while he carried the basket of cherries with the other. He had the look of a man who had made a decision. He knew what he had to do to get his life back on track. The woman cuddling next to him was the answer. Marjorie was everything he needed to complement his life.

Bingo, after finishing his steak bone, came running down the path toward them.

Marjorie was overjoyed that she had made progress in vying for Les' affection. She was merrily strolling along, enjoying her Canadian experience. How could she impress upon Les that she had a feeling that they were predestined to be together? She was hoping the next few days would strengthen his feelings for her, and that he would arrive at the same conclusion. She could only stand by and wait as Les pondered his future.

CHAPTER 36

The next day was Saturday. Les had a meeting with Linda. At Kingsbridge Park for two p.m. Driving to the park, Les went over the possible questions and answers he would have to deal with. He hoped the discussion would remain friendly without creating resentment. Linda was sitting on a park bench near the children's playground, looking drained and weary. She had a forlorn look on her face as though knowing Les had made a decision that was not in her favor. "Hi Linda, how are you?" he asked.

"Life could be better." She gave Les a feint smile, stood up and approached him. Les gave her a quick hug and stepped back.

"Let's take a walk. We'll take the path around the park the same as we used to, shall we?" he suggested. Starting down the flower lined path, past the picnic shelter and over towards the ball fields. They passed a Chinese ethnic group setting up for an afternoon picnic.

Addressing the purpose of the meeting with Linda, Les spoke firs.t "I can only say this one way Linda. I believe that it is best that we not get back together, the affair with Grant would haunt us." He kept gazing at her face to gauge her reaction.

"I can see why you're feeling like that Les. Can we try to get past that? After all, you were away several months. Are you saying there were no women in your life during while with the Navy?"

Les hesitated. "I suppose that's a fair comment Linda. Look, I'm not holding you completely responsible. People are human, with human needs. Few of us lead perfectly virtuous lives. Relationships are similar to rubber bands; you can stretch them, sure. Some will be stretched too far and never regain their shape. That is how I feel about our relationship. It is better for both of us if we just go our separate ways. You'll find someone else." He stopping he turned and facing her.

Looking at him at him with tear filled, sorrowful eyes, she folded. "If that's what you want Les, I have no choice." Turning they walked back to their cars, saying little else. Standing there, Les was recounting the three years of memories with Linda, watching her drive slowly away.

He glanced at the playground and saw children hooting and hollering as they played. They were apparently playing without regard as to what their future might hold in another fifteen years or so. The joys of being a child, he thought returning to his car.

〜〜〜

Marjorie was feeling uncertain as she gathered her sunglasses and sandals together for a walk down to the lobby's business center. She was going to email Sadie, her boss, as she promised. She began,

"Dear Sadie. Here I am five thousand miles from home. Canada is a beautiful country and the tour is going great. I have met that someone. His name is Les. He may just be the person in my dream! I just have to determine whether it is I craving that outcome, or if indeed this is a real chance at connecting with him. I will be informing you as to what happens during the next few days. Love Marjorie."

She was leaving the computer center when her roommate, Judy, approached. "I have bad news and good news, Marjorie," she announced.

Stopping to face her, Marjorie asked. "Judy, is this one of your jokes? Are you serious?"

"No joke Marjorie. The bad news is that Gary, that older person in room 1818, had to fly home. He had to take care of some urgent business matters.

"So, what is the good news?"

"The tour operator said that I could move into Gary's vacant room for the remainder of the time we are here. That means we will each have rooms." She winked at Marjorie.

Marjorie blushing at Judy's inference understood the reason for Judy's joy. They would both be at liberty enjoying the privacy that single hotel rooms offered. "Judy, let me help you move your things," was her instantaneous reply.

Marjorie was thinking about Les. Would this development be providing her with another chance to get Les into the right frame of mind? Would he be interested in taking their budding romance a step further by beginning an intimate relationship? Possibilities were looking up, thought Marjorie. She began daydreaming about the way things might be evolving during the next few days. Les had promised to call her that evening. She was looking forward to seeing him again.

Later that afternoon Marjorie returned to the computer room to see if Sadie had replied. She had.

"Dear Marjorie, I was so pleasing to receive your e-mail and thrilling to learn you may have met the man of your dreams. Matters here at work are much the same as when you left, Mrs. Simpson passed away. As you know, her condition was day to day for the past month. Mr. Rye has taken her room. He is a pleasant man when he is not in his forgetful phase. Keep updating me on your quest and do have a pleasant vacation. I am happy for you. Love Sadie P.S. Keep your eyes peeled for my Mr. Right."

Smiling, Marjorie signed off and hurried to her room, to await Les' call.

Glancing at his watch, Les saw it was three o'clock. He felt re-energized now that his ties with Linda had been completely severed. He had never been fully contented with the relationship. There had always been a nagging feeling lurking in his mind. A future with Linda was not his real destiny. Now he was beginning to understand that feeling. Was Marjorie his true soul mate, the one that he was waiting for? "Destiny."

Reminding himself that Marjorie would be expecting his call, he went to the farm office. Most of the picking activities for the day were over. Closing the door, he dialed the hotel. "Hi Marjorie, how you today?"

"Just fine, Les, I just got in from downstairs .I was e-mailing my supervisor and friend Sadie." Marjorie responded

'That was considerate of you. I'll bet she was glad to hear from you."

"Yes, she wants me to find another guy like you and bring him back to Scotland for her," she said chuckling.

"That should keep you occupied for the remainder of your vacation. Better yet, tell her the bag limit on bachelors in Canada is one per year." Laughing and changed the topic. "Say I thought we would drive over to Toronto to dine and dance."

"Now that sounds sensational. Is it a place you've been to before? What is it like?"

"I've been there once. It's called Captain Matthew Flinders. It's a small cruise ship, operating in Toronto's harbor," he continued. 'We board at eight. Could you be ready by seven?"

"Oh, I'll be ready Les," she continued with a nervous laugh. '"I even have a plans for you later."

"What might that be?" He could sense she was flirting with him.

"It's a midnight surprise. I'll tell you then." She purred.

"Do you turn into a pumpkin?" He teased back.

"Better than that, now, no more guessing. I'll see you at seven." They ended the call. She went to her closet taking out her black evening gown and checking it over before proceeding to shower.

Strolling over to the main house, Les began informing Gloria that he would be going out.

"With your little Scottish friend?" She asked.

"Yes, tonight could be special. We're going on the dinner cruise in Toronto. That one you went on with dad last year, on your anniversary."

"Oh yes, she'll like that! It was a great evening." Gloria added.

"Can I come?" Evelyn asked with a grin on her face showing she was merely joking.

"You can come next time.' Les replied. "Now, I have to get ready" Turning, he and started up the stairs to the bedroom level.

ᵣᵣᵣ

Arriving promptly at eight, Marjorie and Les followed other patrons down the walkway onto the ship. The Flinders was custom built and lavishly outfitted with lush carpeting, warm woods and Danish brass. Marjorie feeling the warmth and intimacy of the interior decks admired the spacious outdoor decks. Guests were preparing to enjoy a dazzling trip along Toronto's harbor front. They were shown to a table on the outdoor deck, to enjoy a cocktail, before being invited indoors for the buffet dinner. Following the dinner was dancing.

"Everything is perfect!" said Marjorie gaping at the lavish surroundings.

Helping her get seated, Les agreed. "They didn't spare anything when converting her to a dinner cruise ship."

A hostess approached their table, placing two glasses on the table. "Hi I'm Cindy, Champagne? Les glanced at Marjorie who was nodding. "Yes, both champagne," he requested.

The hostess began filling the glasses and smiling, "Is this a special occasion for you two?"

Marjorie answered first "I'm over from Scotland. This is my first visit to Canada."

"Well then, that is something special. Enjoy your evening." Cindy turned to attend to the adjoining table.

Marjorie looked stunning in her black evening gown as the sunset started turning into twilight. "A toast, to the best looking woman on board." Les complimented her and raised his glass. He noticed the black pearl necklace again and remembered the history of the jewelry.

"You look very dashing yourself," she replied. They clicked glasses and sipped their drinks. The boat began moving away from the dock. She smiled to herself as she was looking at him. She had plans for Les. They involved more than dining and dancing.

CHAPTER 37

The evening was storybook. In addition to the luxurious relaxing atmosphere, the buffet featuring Atlantic salmon was superb. The desserts in Marjorie's later description "to die for" summed it all up.

Helping themselves to the buffet and taking their seats. Marjorie began exploring Les' likes and dislikes. The background music in the room, prompted her to ask, "What is your favorite music and singer Les?"

"I like Ronnie Stewart and Elvis of course, the Beatles, most songs from way, way back. I could never explain my tastes in music to my friends. How about you Marjorie?"

Smiling, Marjorie responded, "I like Stewart for sure, and the Beatles and Elton John. Much the same as you. I'm not into these new excessively synthesized musical recordings."

"We are getting old in our twenties," He remarked thinking, of his parents with whom he shared many of their tastes in music.

Les found it astounding to learn everything they were talking about was magically interesting to them both. The bond between them grew as they continued exchanging experiences. They found it surprising how they could read each other's thoughts. Neither had experienced such an extraordinary feeling of closeness and kinship.

They took the waitress' suggestion, moving indoors to

the lounge and dance area where the DJ was selecting his evening's music. Selecting a table and sitting beside one another, facing the dance floor and the DJ, Marjorie whispered, "This is cozy!" She slid her body snuggly, against Les. 'Good' she thought. Les didn't appear to mind the closeness. In fact, she was sensing he was enjoying her forwardness.

With the lights dimming, and the music starting with a romantic ballad. Many couples rose to dance. "Marjorie, would you care to dance?" Les said standing and offering his hand to Marjorie.

Reaching out to join him, Marjorie responded, "I would love to." Never giving any thought to the fact this was their first dance. They began moving like dancers who had been together many times. Their bodies came ever closer to each other as they danced down the length of the dance floor. Les did not consider himself an accomplished dancer. With Marjorie as his partner, he could found he could move in response to her every step with smooth movements. The evening hours flew by as they continued enjoying dance after dance. All too soon, the ship was docking. The cruise was over; however, the evening was far from ended.

⌒⌒⌒

Driving back to Niagara Falls with Les, Marjorie was trying to decide how to communicate to Les that she had her own hotel room. Deciding to fit it in to the conversation, she commented as she put her hand on his arm. "That was a delightful evening Les. I really enjoyed every minute."

"The pleasure was all mine. Maybe we can do it again, before you have to leave." He said putting his right arm around her shoulder.

"Let's not talk about my leaving," she suggested. "Can you come up to the room for a coffee when we get back?" She cooed smiling at him, hoping he would accept.

"We had better ask your roommate." Les replied.

She saw her chance. "Actually, I have the room to myself Les. One of our group left this afternoon. My roommate got her own room."

Les didn't hesitate. "Coffee it is then, my friend." Marjorie leaned over and gave him a peck on the cheek. She had prompted him to take the next step in their relationship. She hoped everything would work out the way she had envisioned.

It was one a.m. as they parked in the hotel's parking area and took the elevator up to room 1817.They each carried a Tim Horton's take-out coffee .

Marjorie fumbled nervously with one hand and the key trying to open the door.

"Let me get that." He handed Marjorie his coffee. Taking the key, opening the door, and then stepping aside he let her pass by.

"Want to watch some TV while I freshen up?" She offered him the remote.

He turned it on checking the channel display. He found the "soft music" channel. Switching to it, Les wondered how things would unfold during the next few hours. He was experienced enough to recognize Marjorie's motivation in inviting him to spend the night with her. That was his wish as well. What was concerning Les was the effect, if any, of breaking up with Linda. Would that inhibit his ability to focus his attention on Marjorie?

Coming out of the bathroom dressed in a light pink bathrobe, Marjorie chirruped. "It's your turn," she smiled. "You'll find a man's bathrobe on the back of the bathroom door." Leaning forward she kissed him. Her bathrobe sagged opening up , revealing her bare breasts in the soft glow of the streetlights .

ᘐᘐᘐ

"Too late for that sweetie." Les remarked drawing her to him kissing her fully on the lips and then proceeding to shower her with short demanding kisses to her cheeks, earlobes and the nape of her neck. Marjorie responded returning each of his kisses, her nostrils flaring with excitement as she began breathing rapidly.

Fifty years of pent up passion was suddenly released. Any thought of Les getting a bathrobe was forgotten, as he was losing himself in Marjorie's arms and charms. Feeling her smooth, velvety skin against his face ,he started kissing her breasts. Feeling her nipples hardening, he responded. Gently lifting her, he carried her over to the turned down bed. In two swift motions, his shirt and trousers disappeared over the side of the bed. Drawing the sheets up over their bodies, they lost themselves in each other's arms.

With their desires met and their passions calming, they now knew they had more than minutes. They had hours and days to spend enjoying the pleasures of lovemaking. They were where they belonged. Every passing moment was strengthening their resolve. They where were they wanted to be. At long last, destiny had brought them to-gether, culminating a fifty-year journey.

After searching for contentment and happiness, a solid relationship was developing between them. A relation-ship revolving not only around sexual attraction. It was a meeting of two spirits, reaching in concert like floating white clouds in a summer sky.

The End

ENDING # 2

CHAPTER 38

2075

Dawn broke on a Scottish moor thirty kilometers June 1, east of Aberdeen. Twenty- two year old Marjorie Nichols awakened from a deep sleep. She had just experienced an extremely realistic dream. Marjorie had dreamt that she had travelled to Niagara Falls, Canada where she met her future husband.

The only detail, in the dream, not discernible was his face. When he had turned to greet her, all she saw was a featureless face. He possessed no eyes, no hair color, no eyelashes, no smile, and no facial appearance at all. At that point, she awakened with a shock. "What the hell was that all about?" she muttered. Stumbling, still half asleep, she managed her way to the bathroom.

The dream did not fade into her sub-conscious, as most dreams do. She remembered she had been looking at the travel ads the previous night in the "Aberdeen Independent." Advertised in there was a special tour of Eastern Canada, including a week's stay at Niagara Falls, Ontario.

"That's where it came from," she decided, thinking back to the subject matter of that morning's dream. She brushed her red auburn hair and applied makeup to her slightly freckled face. Taking a high liner brow pencil, she touched up her eyebrows. Her hazel eyes liked what she saw, as she looked at her reflection in the mirror. She was looking forward to the day. Would it be one of those life changing days that happen to people perhaps once in a lifetime? Would something occur that would guide the wheels of her future wagon along the right path?

Throughout the day, while working, as a nurse, at the local long-term care facility, her mind kept reexamining the dream. The reference to Niagara Falls was dominating her thoughts, as she started her shift.

During her lunch hour, she went to the travel agency that had advertised the tour. It was only a short distance from her place of work. The pigeonhole travel office was crammed between a bank and a liquor store. Staffing the shop was one clerk, who was reading a McCall's magazine.

Springing to her feet at the prospect of making a sale to Marjorie, she put down the magazine smiling. "Welcome to Travel's Unlimited." She said in a low and lust voice, "I'm Heather, how may I help you?" She said rising from her seat.

"Good afternoon, I'm Marjorie." Reaching into her purse, withdrawing and unfolding the newspaper page she was carrying in her purse, Marjorie drew attention to ad from the 'Independent'." I was reading this ad about your Canadian tour; can you provide me more information about this trip?"

Heather reached behind her for a brochure. She turned to face Marjorie. "Have a seat," she answered. She unfolded the brochure. "That's a very popular excursion. In fact we have only five tickets left for the June 24th to July

15th tour. The next one isn't until September, for the fall colors in Algonquin Park." She proceeded to show Marjorie the full itinerary of the tour starting in St. John's Newfoundland, proceeding to the Maritimes, Quebec City, Ottawa, and ending in Niagara Falls, Ontario.

Marjorie's pulse quickened at the thought of travelling to Canada. "I do have three weeks of paid vacation for this year." Making up her mind, she continued. "Yes, I will book the Niagara Tour." Marjorie could not remember when she had been so decisive. She felt a compelling need to travel to Niagara Falls. It was, as if this was a necessary undertaking along her life path.

She completed booking the trip, with a keen sense of calm satisfaction. Back at work, she advised the pay mistress of her holiday plans. "Sadie, I'm off to Canada for three weeks starting June 22nd."

Sadie responded, appearing surprised. "When did you decide that?" She had been encouraging Marjorie to use up her vacation time. In fact, she had mentioned it just a few days earlier.

Marjorie excitedly related the details of her dream. Sadie took a lively interest in how precisely Marjorie was recalling each facet of the dream.

Marjorie concluded by saying. "Perhaps I'll meet Mr. Right in Niagara Falls." The more she kept talking about the trip, the more convinced she was that it was the right decision.

They agreed she could return any time, if her plans for Canada did not work out. Sadie teased her. "It should be the trip of a lifetime," Sadie added. "If you do meet your Mr. Right, do you mind asking him if he has an older unattached brother for me?" She laughed at the serious look Marjorie gave her. "You're really into this aren't you?"

"It just feels so right," replied Marjorie, smiling and flicking the hair out of her face. "The more I think about it the more excited I am about going." Beaming, Marjorie turned and walked down the hall to begin her duties on the ward. Was this trip to Canada the start of something new and long lasting? The future would hold the answer to that. By going on this trip, was she taking the first step in finding her lifetime partner?

CHAPTER 39

At Niagara on the Lake, Les Schwab a Navy seaman from Victoria B.C., was helping his parents on their family orchard. It was his way of spending his yearly holidays, as well as visiting his parents. He was unattached, not yet ready to settle down to married life. The Navy was his passion. He had not taken time to develop a lasting relationship. Les had made it a ritual to spend the period from June 15 to July 31 in the Niagara Falls area. He could not explain why he chose those dates. In fact, the major part of the farm work occurred later in the year.

At dinner that evening, his mother asked him for a favor. "Your Uncle William is coming down from Toronto on the long weekend. Your cousin Evelyn, from Winnipeg, will also be in town for a few days. She wants to see Niagara Falls. Would you mind showing them around? You and Evelyn were always close when you were youngsters."

"I like Evelyn. Sure it will be great to see her again." Les recalled the tomboy cousin he had hung out with during summer holidays. He hadn't seen her for several years.

"Would you take them out for a few hours on July 1? Willie likes to watch the fireworks at Niagara Falls. He doesn't get out much since his motorcycle accident is confining him to a wheel chair. Too bad, He is so young to be 31 and in that situation."

"Is he improving?" Les questioned, as his mother was reminding him of his Uncle Willie's plight.

"His therapy is coming along fine. He can stand and walk short distances now. He thinks he will be recovering fully in six months. They're holding his mechanic's job for him at the motorcycle dealership.

Nodding, Les answered. "Good for him, he was their best worker! I enjoy Willie and Evelyn. I'll take them wherever they want to go."

Les continually went to Niagara falls on July first of every year. It was a regular event. He had no explanation for his action. It was as though someone was beckoning him to a rendezvous at the Falls.

The long weekend came. Les, Evelyn and Willie were waiting for the gathering dusk and the start of the fireworks. Willie parking his wheel chair near the rail was admiring the falls from the viewing deck. Les had brought four folding chairs so he could put one on either side of Willie. That would ensure Willie would not be jostled by the growing crowd.

The time for the fireworks display neared. A young, freckle faced, auburn haired young woman began approaching them. Breaking away from a tour bus crowd, she was glancing their way. Then instinctively turning and coming within a few feet of Les and Willie. Her face lit up she appeared to be recognizing them. Les saw Willie showing a keen interest in her. "Do either of you gentlemen have the time?" she inquired. She was standing there, smiling and whipping the auburn hair out of her face in the slight breeze.

'Hardly a new approach' Les was thinking, as he gave her the once over. She was in her early twenties, he guessed. Her auburn hair was probably a conversion from a youthful head of carrot-red hair. Her face was sprinkled liberally with freckles. Her smile was infectious. She had on a white top with red and white striped shorts and carried a blue nylon shell jacket. Around her neck, she wore a black pearl necklace.

Les had a recollection about a black pearl necklace, He knew he had seen it somewhere before. Les finally decided that he must have seen a similar necklace at some movie or other. By her Scottish accent, Les was assuming she was an overseas tourist.

Gathering his thoughts first, Les answered. "It's almost ten. You're just in time." He returned her smile, locking eyes with her.

Blushing lightly, but without flinching, she returned Les' smile. "Thank you; by the way my name is Marjorie." She elaborated. "Marjorie Nichols, I'm visiting from Scotland."

"Hi Marjorie, I'm Les Schwab and this is my cousin Evelyn." He gave Marjorie a grin, adding. "This is Willie, my uncle."

"Hi Willie," Marjorie showed no hesitation in extending her hand to him, Willie readily accepting.

Marjorie turned back to Les, smiling broadly, as their hands met. Les again sensing she was an acquaintance from his past. Marjorie was gazing into his eyes as though Les looked familiar to her as well. Her eyes shone with happiness, as though her mind was also search for a connection. Was this the man from her dream?

Motioning to the empty seat, Les said. "We have an extra place here Marjorie; you're welcome to join us."

Releasing Les' hand, and taking the seat, she replied. "Well, yes I will. Thank you for the invitation Les."

Glancing at his watch, Les noted. "It will be another half hour before the fireworks. Tell us about your trip Marjorie. What prompted you to come to Canada?" He was hoping something in her words would answer the vexing feeling he had about them having met somewhere.

With some elaborate detail, she began explaining her dream and the later travel advertisement in the local paper back home, followed by her decision to book the trip. "I've had a great time on the tour. We've seen the Maritimes, parts of Quebec and now Ontario. We spent two days in Algonquin Park, a glorious place. Now we are here in Niagara Falls for three days." Chuckling she continued. "If this keeps up, I may be finding that job and immigrating here."

As she was elaborating, Les looked for any clues that would place her in his life in his past. Marjorie was mentioning that she had a great aunt, Elizabeth who had lived on Vancouver Island, for a short while with her sister Lisa. When Lisa died, Clara, Marjorie's mother, was given the black pearl necklace.

That triggered a faint memory in Les, remembering that he had a great uncle on Vancouver Island. He had met a premature death. There was a chance that Marjorie's great aunt and Les' great uncle had known each other. Les started explaining his reasoning to Marjorie.

Evelyn spoke up with her opinion "I think what we

may have here is a clear case of reincarnation. You have both come back within your own families and here you are reliving your lives in a new location".

Willie scoffing at the explanation, interjected. "That's a fairy tale that's springing from your overworked imagination Evelyn." He began waving his hand as if fending off a fly. "You may as well say you met in Mars!"

Marjorie, on the other hand, furling her eyebrows and listening intently to Les and Evelyn. She was warming up to the suggestion of reincarnation as being a logical explanation of her dream. The fact they both had faint memories of having met before, was reinforcing the notion.

Evelyn's comments reminded Marjorie of what she had read about reincarnation claims. Many of the reports appeared to be more than credible. She described a case of a nine-year-old girl killed in an accident in England. In addition, a few years later she was reborn in a nearby area. When she was nine their family visited a neighboring village that she recognized as her former home. She could go directly to the house where she had lived in her prior life. She knew her parents and aunt by name.

The theory made sense to Les and Marjorie; however, with Willie's continued scoffing and after gazing in each other's eyes Les suggested. "We'll have to talk about that at greater length later."

Marjorie nodded agreement, realizing a three way discussion on the subject was futile.

As the evening progressed, Marjorie warmed up to Willie and they exchanged stories about nursing. She from the practitioner's standpoint and he from the two years of having been confined to a hospital bed. Marjorie found him interesting. She felt empathy for his handicap, since she worked in the rest home industry. Willie invited her to visit the lodge where he lived. He was certain they needed a nurse for the afternoon shift.

Marjorie found the suggestion interesting, agreeing to follow up on the position. "Sure, I'll look into it Willie. If I don't, I may be missing out on something that could change my future for the better."

"That sounds like a win, win plan," Les said somewhat unenthusiastically. He kept gazing out over the falls. pondering his future. He was somewhat resentful at Willie's interest in Marjorie. Why should he feel that way? He had only met Marjorie less than an hour ago. What was triggering these possessive feelings in him? There was more at play here than just his fleeting attraction towards Marjorie. Would this woman be impacting his life by Marjorie's decision to relocate to Canada?

This enthusiastic ball of Scottish fire had him entranced. He could not help himself as he looked at her only. Marjorie immediately noticed the attention and smiled invitingly whenever their eyes met.

The fireworks began. People were jostling for position along the waterfront rails so they could get a firsthand look at the spectacular exploding patterns. Every minute or two, dazzling displays of lights and sounds erupted, to the delight of the spectators.

Marjorie motioned to Les and they stood up and walked a few feet back from the railing to a less crowded area. "Willie seems very charming. May I ask how he got injured?" she said trying to be casual about the chance meeting.

"It happened about two years ago. We were both entered in a motocross motorcycle competition and another bike came down on Willie, when he wiped out. I was a few seconds behind and I was sent flying as well. Luckily I was not seriously injured, just a few scratches and bruises. For a few weeks, we thought Willie would be remaining paralyzed. He's taking extensive therapy and is hoping to be walking in a few months. The doctors say he needs some kind of motivation to get him working harder on his rehab."

"Well then, let's find him a woman friend." Suggested Marjorie as she winked at Les.

Les ,thinking that Marjorie was found Willie interesting, replied. "He obviously has taken a liking to you Marjorie!" Les had to force himself to say those words. Something inside of him said, you fool, don't be so stand-offish for goodness sake. He continued "That would be very kind of you; it may just get him thinking positive again." Though disappointed by the turn of events, Les was pleased with the fact that Marjorie considered taking time to help a complete stranger. It showed compassion, a trait that reminded him of his mother. It made him even more attracted to her.

Marjorie turned and took Les' arm as they walked back toward Willie. She noticing the downcast mood Les was unable to hide. Reaching over with her other hand and placed it in on Les' arm. "Not me, silly, I have a supervisor named Sadie. She may find him the perfect person for her. I will suggest to Willie that they start e-mailing. You never can tell what may develop between them."

Les felt reassured. Fate had blessed him. He reached

around Marjorie's shoulders and drew her nearer to him. He now realized, the matchless beauty of this spirited woman was what may have beckoned him back year after year to Niagara Falls. "Say Marjorie if you can book tomorrow off, we can take the boat tour of the falls instead, how about it?"

"Sure," she agreed, "our group will be taking the boat tour in the morning. I can wait for mine until mid afternoon as we have no further outings after two o'clock."

"Where are you staying?" he prompted her.

"We're lodging at the Oakes Hotel, on the U.S side, room 1817," she said suggestively.

"Fine, I'll pick you up shortly after two."

༞

Marjorie arrived back at the hotel. After showering and getting into clean attire, she sent Sadie an e-mail.

"Dear Sadie.

Here I am five thousand miles from home. Canada is a beautiful country and the tour is going great. I have met that someone. His name is Les. He may just be the person about whom I dreamt. I just have to determine whether it is I craving that outcome, or if indeed this is a real chance at connecting with a soul mate.

We are meeting again tomorrow. I will keep you informed as to what happens in the next few days.

By the way, Les has a 33-year-old uncle, William, who has expressed an interest in corresponding with you. I think you and he could explore the possibility of meeting. He is recovering from a motorcycle accident. He expects to be back at work in six months or so. Give me the green light and I will give him your e-mail. I think the therapeutic value of him having someone to correspond with would do him wonders.

Love Marjorie."

CHAPTER 40

The "Maid of the Mist III "was overloading its' 130 person capacity. In fact, the operator of the boat, Captain Stuart, had been making a habit of allowing 30 more passengers than permitted to board the small vessel, easing the back-log of waiting passengers.

Marjorie and Les were waiting to board. Marjorie with Les in tow was working her way to the front of the pier to get a better view. Seeing space on the dock rail, she moved forward and squeezing them into an opening be-side a man in his late twenties and a woman in her late fifties. "Pardon me for pushing in," she said apologizing, as she secured her place. "This is my first tour of the Falls." Les glancing over at her was admiring her persistence and eagerness, as well as her appearance. Marjorie's hair, a dark shade of auburn, was fluttering in the wind. Her face had a liberal sprinkling of freckles. Her smile was contagious.

"It's quite alright," responded the stranger, making room for her. "You will always remember your first visit to Niagara Falls."

It was 2.45 P.M. The passengers were boarding the vessel for the 3 P.M. sailing. The crew were handing a hooded raincoats to the passengers to protect them from the spray.

"Do I look like a fish monger? " Marjorie quipped, as Les was helping her with the bulky coat.

"If you are, then you're a mighty pretty one." Les replied complimenting her and winking as he was donning his raincoat. They made their way to the front of the "Mist" to get an unobstructed view of the Falls. Marjorie locking arms with Les, felt secure knowing she had the support of someone who had been on the boat before. She had the sensation of "deva vu" as they began walking forward.

The Falls boat tour was to take 45 minutes. People on board were waving to those left behind. The vessel pulled out into the Niagara Basin, propelling forward, towards the spray and thunderous roar of the falls. The sounds were intensifying as the boat neared the falls. Spray was drenching everyone as the Mist closed the distance.

The "Maid" was about fifty yards from the closest point to the Falls. A large spruce tree stump came rocketing down the Niagara river, over the falls, and slamming broadside into the front side of the "Maid". People were thrown headlong into the water The sudden jolt interrupting the forward progress of the vessel with a tremendous force. With the vessel's moment halting, the tour boat began lurching off balance at a 45-degree angle, tossing passenger overboard. Amongst them were Les and Marjorie.

Les, being a trained Navy diver, kept his wits about him as he was surfacing. Being an expert swimmer, he wasn't in any danger. Slipping out of the raincoat and waiting for rescuing, he was glancing around, looking for persons faltering. Amidst the screams of other passengers and thrashing bodies around him, he spotted Marjorie a few feet away. She was in some difficulty, being bogged down by the heavy raincoat. She was barely able to keep her head up. Les swam over lifting her under her arms and turning her on her back , face up.

Les kept reassuring her. "Just relax Marjorie, I've got you. You'll be fine." Life buoys began landing in the water to their right. Within a few minutes, they were safely in a Zodiac rescue boat that had sped over to the area.

Shivering and frightened Marjorie clung to Les. "I'm not sure I would have made it without your help," She said, with teeth chattering, as she began snuggling up against him.

Drawing her nearer to him, he minimized his role. "I'm glad I could help, think nothing of it.," he continued. "Actually, I'm pleased we came even under these circumstances."

"I'll second that." Raising her head, Marjorie looked squarely at Les. Smiling broadly, she snuggled closer.

"Are we considering this a date?" Les asked, teasing her. They laughed simultaneously at their present circumstances huddling, dripping wet, in the corner of the rescue boat.

"Well, that was some way of meeting! Yes, I would agree it is our second date." Marjorie joked snuggling against the warmth of Les' body. "I hope we will have a few more!" she added.

Les was feeling a closeness developing between them. Now that he had met Marjorie, he was beginning to realize why he had been coming to the falls year after year.

"Marjorie, would you join me for dinner this evening?" He asked surprising himself at his own forwardness.

Marjorie grinned ,accepting without hesitation, and reminding him . "You know the room number, 1817."

"I'll be there at seven." Les replied, while assisting up the stairs to the pier. They walked to the waiting area where people were the tour operators were offering free taxi rides to passengers.

Perhaps, I was right, dreams do come true, thought Marjorie as she was waving to Les through the cab window.

The End.

CHAPTER 41

2110

It was a crisp October day in Niagara Falls. Les Schawb had just retired from the Canadian Navy and was enjoying his life on the family farm near Niagara On The Lake. His wife of 38 years, Judy, was with him. They decided to visit Legion Branch # 396, on Legion Street, for a noon luncheon. They arrived at 12.15 p.m. The Legion was alive with conversation and happy diners.

The last remaining two seats were at a table for four, already occupied by Brian and Marjorie Nichols. Brian had just retired from the R.C.M Police and they had recently moved from Ottawa to Niagara.

Sheldon, the Legion manager welcomed Les and Judy. He, then escorted them over to meet Brian and Marjorie.

"Brian and Marjorie I would like you to meet Les and Judy."

As Les touched Marjorie's hand, the most unusual sensation swept through him, as though he had met Marjorie before. Their eyes locked in mutual recognition. As his gaze dropped, he noticed the black pearl necklace that graced her neck.

A feeling of familiarity passed through his body. He

knew he was reliving something from his past. "I'm very pleased to meet you Marjorie. I expect we will be seeing you here from time to time. After all it's quite a small city."

She smiled affectionately and fluttering her eyelashes at him, responding to his warm seemingly familiar touch. "I'm sure we will Les. Yes I agree it's a small city in a small world."

Judy and Brian looking somewhat bewildered, began exchanging nervous smiles as they all took their seats.

The End.

17445846R00127

Made in the USA
Charleston, SC
11 February 2013